DISRUPTION BY DESIGN

For Mid-Career Professionals Ready to Choose Design Over Default

Tina Schaaf

DISRUPTION BY DESIGN: For Mid-Career Professionals Ready to Choose Design Over Default

Published by: Executive Books | Tremendous Life Books

P.O. Box 267, Boiling Springs,
PA 17007 717-701-8159 | 800-233-2665

www.TremendousLeadership.com

Every effort has been made to ensure the accuracy and integrity of the information presented in this book. To protect client confidentiality, names and identifying details have been changed. The integrity of each client's journey has been preserved. The author and publisher disclaim any liability for errors, omissions, or outcomes resulting from the use of this material. This book is intended for informational and inspirational purposes only and is not a substitute for professional advice.

Printed in the United States of America

First Edition

Paperback ISBN: 978-1-961202-78-8
eBook ISBN: 978-1-961202-79-5

TABLE OF CONTENTS

ACKNOWLEDGMENTS

To the Reader

Congratulations as you step forward to *disrupt default* and allow me to guide you to re*design* who you are becoming. But more importantly, *thank you*. Writing *Disruption by Design* was not just an act of creativity—it was a calling. And if this book has stirred something inside of you, then mission accomplished. My deepest hope is that every chapter, every elevation exercise, and every story meets you where you are, and pushes you just far enough to disrupt what no longer serves you.

To My Clients

You are the heartbeat of this message. Your bravery, your willingness to be seen, to get uncomfortable, to rewrite what's possible—*this* is what inspires every tool, framework, and insight within these pages. Thank you for trusting me to walk beside you as your Executives Agent™. It has been an honor to witness your rise.

To My Family

To my husband, Peter—your belief in me when I doubted myself was the wind in my sails. Your commitment and love are cherished. You gave strength when I questioned the value of my voice. To my Mother (Jan), Bonus Dad (Jerry), and Auntie Marlene —your faith, support, encouragement, and love are priceless. And to my children—thank you for reminding me of what truly matters. You are my reason, my grounding, and my greatest teachers in legacy and love.

To My Mentors and Guides

To those who lit the path ahead—known and unknown—your wisdom echoes in these pages. From the eternal truth of my Savior, Jesus Christ, to the wisdom of mentors like John Lynch, and the inspiration of leaders like Martin Luther King Jr., Amelia Earhart, Simon Sinek, Tony Robbins, and many others—your influence helped shape this work.

To the Dreamers, Disruptors, and Doers

This book is not just about transformation; it's about becoming *whole*. You are not broken. You are not behind. You are not too late. Everything you need is already within you. You were not designed for the default path. You were designed—fearfully, wonderfully—for a life that reflects your truth, your strengths, and your divine purpose.

PUBLISHER'S FOREWORD
by Tracey C. Jones, PhD

There are moments in publishing when you know a book will matter. It's not about trends or metrics. You sense it the moment you meet an author and feel something beyond business. That's exactly what happened when I met Tina Schaaf.

I spoke at a Convene gathering, a peer advisory group for Christian CEOs, in Phoenix, AZ. Tina sat to my right. The moment we met, I knew she was a kindred spirit. As CEOs shared their goals, Tina's words stood out with a clarity that became a hallmark of this book. She said, simply and firmly, that God told her to stop playing small.

After the session, she told me something unforgettable. She had nearly stayed home, not feeling her best and wanting to show up with excellence. But something compelled her. She called it providence. So do I.

We stayed in touch. I had her on my leadership podcast. Over time, I saw an emerging message she had long carried. After a series of Holy Spirit prompts, Tina shared her work on this book. It had germinated for years and was ready for harvest. She sought the right publishing partner. I thank God she chose Tremendous Leadership.

I say that not just as a publisher, but as someone who needed this message. I have had many career disruptions—from active-duty military service to semiconductors to defense contracting to federal government contracting. Finally, I ended up running a second-generation international leadership company. Most disruptions hit me like a ton of bricks. Looking back, I realize most pivots were driven by pain, not purpose.

When I read Tina's manuscript, something shifted. I realized how much power I had all along. God was making me lean into His calling, if I just respected His design. This book does the same. It helps you navigate the chaos of our work and its purpose, guiding you with clarity, conviction, and confidence.

What you hold is the result of Tina's journey through her own career transitions. She developed and applied every framework in this book firsthand, then refined them by guiding leaders who chose to stop defaulting and start designing.

My father, Charlie "Tremendous" Jones, championed a simple truth: you will be the same person in five years as you are today, except for the people you meet and the books you read. This is one of those books. And Tina is one of those people.

Read it. Apply it. Let it disrupt you—by design.

Tracey C. Jones, PhD
President, Tremendous Leadership

FOREWORD
by John Lynch

Imagine disruption as a person pulling up beside you as you stand, startled, at a new and daunting crossroads.

He might call out from the driver's seat through the rolled-down passenger window, "Yep, it's me. I know—not who you were hoping for. No problem. I get it all the time. But hear me out for a moment. First, if I'm being honest, you look a little wobbly. Like something you can't quite name suddenly dropped out from under you. Just a bit ago, you were in normal and predictable. Now, nothing feels very sturdy.

"Also, look around and notice where you are. You're at a crossroads. *Your* particular crossroads. Funny thing about crossroads. Almost never is anyone looking for one. But a crossroads—and most often *only* a crossroads—can take you *here*. 'Here' is away from an outgrown, pale, outdated existence to a new, richer life that's been waiting for you. So, although it doesn't feel like it, you, my friend, are in a pretty exciting place. But nothing really changes without disruption. And—voilà—that's why I'm here. I'm not going anywhere for a bit. So, you might want to put me to use in the meantime."

He thumps the passenger seat and looks directly into your eyes. "So, do you want to get in? This could be one very exceptional ride."

...And maybe, this time, because what you have been trying has not been working, you find yourself getting in.

Hello. I'm John Lynch. In 2011, I met Tina Schaaf at a conference. She describes it as a time of "a pivotal realignment into my purpose." Since then, Tina has influenced leaders with authentic, transferable wisdom and direction-changing freedom. It has truly been a disruption by design.

The subtitle describes that this book is for "Mid-Career Professionals Ready to Choose Design Over Default." It is well named. If you find yourself, for whatever reason, at a career crossroads, I don't know of a book that can better prepare you for a fresh season of strength, direction, freedom, realignment, clarity, and new sight.

I can't think of many who would not deeply benefit from *Disruption by Design*. All of us—parents, students, coaches, aviators, bank tellers, even mid-career professionals—come to crossroads. These moments can feel destructive and frightening. They threaten to disrupt our controlled sameness. And we have grown to like that sameness. Most of us would rarely choose anything that might disrupt it.

Disruption always comes with crossroads. Yet, only by embracing disruption at a crossroads can we step into exceptional new possibilities.

As Tina promises, "The most meaningful chapters of our lives rarely begin with clarity. They begin with curiosity. Disruption is uncomfortable. It dismantles your familiar identity. But it also reveals the layers you've outgrown."

Tina asked me to read this book and consider writing the foreword. I was curious why she'd want me, an author and speaker, to write a foreword designed primarily for mid-career professionals. Then I started reading Tina's deeply hopeful, insightful, imaginative wisdom. As soon as I finished, I almost involuntarily bolted out of my office, wanting someone to share in my excitement. A friend, staying with us, was reading in a chair. I blurted out my excitement and strongly told her, "If you know anyone going through any career or life change, you must go get this book for them. Now!" She responded, "Ok. Where can I get it?" "Oh yeah. Well, it's not exactly out yet. But still."

Sincerely, this book has stunned me with its fresh answers to some of life's hardest questions. It is a rare and surprising goodness that a book written for those on a career track could teach this much about the human heart. It has personally drawn me into curiosity about the unsettling but stirring hope of what God may be up to in my story.

As a faith writer, speaker, and pastor, I talk a lot about hiding. Many of us can spend much of our entire lives hiding. We hide from whatever threatens to prove we may not be enough. There may be no greater fear than the thought that we are not enough. Our hiding can take the form of posturing, bluffing, pretending, or faking it. It can cause us to create our own unique masks—masks desperately attempting to convince others that we are enough. It all shouts that we are talented, we have worth, we are important. But we can have a hard time believing it ourselves. We are hiding from an imagined inadequacy we've never allowed ourselves to examine.

Until then, we keep grinding, staying in careers that maybe have never fit us. And we are getting so tired.

Then the day we feared most. Something happens that seems to prove what we suspected all along. Maybe you blow the SATs. Or a fiancé, who's known you a long time, suddenly leaves. Maybe you are a victim of downsizing or an unwanted career change.

It is a great gift to be compelled to face that fear, only so we can discover that maybe the real me, behind the mask, has been enough all along.

Tina gives us the gift of describing her crossroads, where disruption allowed her to enter into a life that was trying to evolve. "...I sat across from a trusted leader and mentor and finally admitted, 'I don't know who I am without the doing.' He looked at me gently and said, 'Tina, you are enough. You don't need to perform perfectly all the time. You are enough, just as you are.' That conversation cracked something open in me. Through that opening came grace—the quiet, steady voice of God, not condemning but inviting."

She declares that was not a breakdown, but a breakthrough trying to begin.

"That was the moment the transformation began. I started peeling back the layers of performance. I got honest about my limits. I let go of the need to impress and started practicing what it meant to be true—to be my true identity. It wasn't clean or easy. Transformation rarely is. It required trust, surrender, humility, and the courage to unlearn. But that was the year I began leading from identity, not image, and that changed everything."

So, back to us. What if, instead of fearing this disruption, we choose to see it as an opportunity at this crossroads? This book is for you if you find yourself where you did not expect to be. Maybe you feel called to make a shift and realign with your purpose. A valuable new normal, full of wonder and goodness, is waiting for you.

You are ready—and fully enough—to step boldly into what comes next.

ENDORSEMENTS

Disruption by Design

"You can be successful in the marketplace even though you're misaligned with what you're truly designed to do and be. But it's just a matter of time before the upside of success can't offset the lack of purpose, satisfaction, energy, and joy you'd prefer to be feeling. If that's you, I've got good news. Her name is Tina Schaaf. Her book is entitled Disruption by Design."

Dr. Tim Kimmel
Author of Grace Based Parenting

"In a world that tells leaders to hustle harder and climb faster, Tina Schaaf offers a radically different invitation: stop, listen, and design from the inside out. Your identity is not defined by your title or your last promotion—it's defined by who you were created to be. This book is a gift to every leader ready to answer that call."

John Christianson
CEO, Highland Private Wealth Management

The professional world is harder to navigate right now than it has been in a long time. AI is changing what jobs look like and which ones survive. Economic uncertainty is real. Most career books were written for a different era. This one was not.

When I first worked with Tina Schaaf, I was navigating an unplanned career change while helping my family care for my aging father. Tina did not give me a formula or a pep talk. She guided me through a process that helped me understand my strengths, clarify what I truly wanted, and move forward with conviction.

In the years since, I have returned to Tina for counsel on job offers, positioning, and high-stakes conversations. She shows up the same way every time: honest, insightful, and deeply committed to helping you find the truth of who you are. She does not just tell you what you want to hear. She asks the questions that get you to the truth.

Disruption by Design brings that same approach to the page. It is thoughtful, practical, and deeply relevant for anyone at a crossroads in their career. In a time when so much is changing, knowing who you are and what you stand for is not a soft skill. It is the most practical thing you can have. This book will help you figure out where you want to go—and how to move forward with clarity.

Tina Schaaf is the kind of guide who changes the outcome. This book makes her wisdom available to everyone who needs it.

Mary Lee Sharp
Global CHRO, Board Member, and Attorney
Advising CEOs, boards of public, P/E, and nonprofit organizations across financial services, insurance, technology & medtech

"In a culture addicted to hustle and performance, Tina Schaaf asks the question most leaders are afraid to answer: Who were you actually created to be? This book is not theory—it's a mirror. And for anyone who has achieved success on the outside while quietly losing themselves on the inside, it offers something far more valuable than strategy: it offers a way home."

Ceitci Demirkova
Founder & CEO, Changing a Generation
Bestselling & Award-Winning Author,
Motivated by the Impossible

Tina Schaaf has a rare ability to meet people at the crossroads of uncertainty and guide them toward clarity, confidence, and purpose. In Disruption by Design, she captures this beautifully reminding us that what feels like a crisis may actually be a calling, and that true transformation begins when we pause long enough to ask who we are becoming.

I have had the privilege of knowing Tina for many years, participating with her in a business forum, and engaging with The Schaaf Group professionally. Each interaction has been marked by depth, insight, and real results.

This book is more than a framework—it is an invitation. An invitation to stop settling, to rediscover alignment, and to build a life that reflects who you were truly created to be.

Jerry R. Meek
Founder & CEO, Desert Star Construction, Inc.

"I've known Tina Schaaf for nearly two decades, and what sets her apart is the same quality that makes this book exceptional: she sees people with a clarity they often can't see in themselves. This isn't theory. It's the distillation of real work with real leaders who were brave enough to stop performing and start designing."

Dan Kristiansen

President, Tricor Strategies, LLC

"Disruption by Design" is the book I wish I'd had during my own seasons of professional transition. Like most in our professional career, I've had a couple pivots. While they were all intentional and guided by convictions, they weren't done with a framework. Then I met Tina—she is finally taking the principles she walked me through and has put these into a valuable resource. She has created a rare framework that is both deeply personal and strategically rigorous.

Jeff Rogers

Chair, Park Place LTD / Chair, OneAccord

"In a world that constantly pushes leaders to achieve more, Tina Schaaf offers a much-needed invitation to pause and realign from within. As a founder and CEO, I've experienced how easily outward success can outpace inner clarity. This book is a thoughtful and grounding guide for leaders navigating seasons of transition—helping them rediscover alignment, strength, and a deeper sense of who they are created to be."

Vivian Yin

Founder & CEO | Y+X Entertainment

INTRODUCTION

How did I get here?

It's a question many people ask themselves at certain seasons of life. Sometimes it surfaces quietly, while sitting in a boardroom debating the title of the next slide in a presentation deck. Sometimes it arrives more abruptly, while stuck in traffic after an all-company meeting where the CEO has just announced the company has been sold and roles will become redundant. Or more recently it surfaced when you walked into the office and noticed new iPad Minis sitting on desks performing tasks that your colleague was responsible for and today, he or she is gone, and AI has replaced their position. In those moments, a simple yet unsettling question arises: *How did I get here—and what comes next?*

During the twelfth year of my business, The Schaaf Group, my focus was on executive recruiting, coaching, and consulting. I had relocated to Arizona while maintaining a presence in Seattle. On an ordinary business day, I paused, struck by the thought: "*Is this it? Will I do this indefinitely?*" In Chapter 2 we will explore this further, at the Professional Crossroads.

Nothing was inherently missing. I wasn't unsatisfied. I just felt a nudge that said, "*You are meant for more.*" Playing small was no longer an option. I needed to develop a way to reach a larger and broader audience than my calendar could currently handle.

That was the moment I chose to answer the ***call*** to shift and realign with my purpose.

This prompting led me on a journey to seek out those who have gone before me and created dynamic, meaningful change. And let me be clear: I am not trying to be anyone else. I have my own experience, skills, methods, and offerings to share. That's the very reason I picked up the book I started a decade ago, brushed it off, recalibrated for a decade of advancement, and finished it.

Many people arrive, like I did, in a quiet yet uncomfortable space where they feel disconnected, possibly directionless, and afraid of the future, yet they can't quite name it. It's not always dramatic, though sometimes it is. It might be a subtle drift, an environmental shift, a forced career change, or just a fog that whispers: "I don't know who I am anymore. What is the meaning of all this? Where do I go from here?"

This place isn't failure. It's not burnout. It's a hidden threshold that can lead to a new future.

Today, with over 14 years as an executive coach and over 20 years as a headhunter, I keep hearing the same things from the people I encounter. They were tired, disenchanted, fearful, or burned out. They lacked clarity about who they were and where they were going. At the core, they had a deep yearning to answer: "Who am I? Why am I unfulfilled? Why am I fearful about the future?"

The answer to these questions starts with a foundation, just like building a house.

I have been fortunate to work with hundreds of executives through their next life and career transitions. I've watched them move from uncertainty, ambiguity, and fear into clarity, confidence, and purpose. They stopped chasing the next "job" and started building lives and careers aligned with who they truly are.

So many of these professionals have gone on to start their own companies, change their career focus entirely, transform their approach to life and relationships, or set up foundations to serve their communities. Over the years many of them told me, "There should be a way to clone you so you could touch more lives."

This book is my answer.

It's my way to honor the gifts I believe are God-given: to truly see people, empower them, share truth, guide them, and help those who desire the opportunity to move into the greatest version of who they were created to be.

My fulfillment comes from guiding mid-career professionals who lack clarity through a process of discovery. This process is the *Disruption by Design*™ framework, and it includes three key steps: First, you gain CLARITY by deeply rediscovering who you are—your values, strengths, and aspirations, to then reimagine what's possible. Next, you CLAIM your "I AM"—owning your strengths (your unique identity), and purpose to create your next move on purpose with confidence. Finally, you

COMMIT to take bold aligned action toward your future possibilities with courage. These steps are the foundation for meaningful and lasting change.

If you are one of those people (and you likely are because you're reading this book), welcome. I am excited to have you on board as we begin your reawakening into an exciting new season of your life.

Work through this book chapter by chapter. Each one builds on the last, and each includes homework to help you truly absorb what you're learning. I've also included client stories throughout to show you this process in action.

I would love to hear how this book has helped you. Visit my website (https://theexecutivesagent.com) to share your story—your feedback matters and can inspire others on their journey.

Now, let's dive in and take the first step toward transforming your career—and your life—by committing fully to this journey. Let's begin now.

Section One: Clarify

GAIN CLARITY BY DEEPLY UNDERSTANDING YOURSELF

Chapter 1

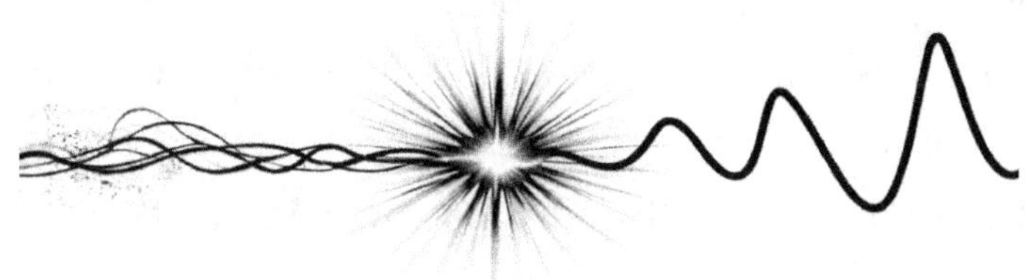

CAREER FOG: WHAT YOU'RE FEELING IS REAL

"Not all those who wander are lost."

—J.R.R. Tolkien

Welcome to the Fog

If you are from the Seattle area, as I am, fog is all too familiar. But fog can be a doorway to something beautiful. Even when it covers everything for a moment in time, there is potential for something amazing waiting on the other side.

I remember standing at Snoqualmie Falls on a calm, foggy evening. The lookout pavilion was completely engulfed. I couldn't see the falls, yet I could hear them. I had been there before, so I knew the beauty that would appear when the fog lifted. Even though I couldn't see it, I could picture it clearly.

This scene mirrors what many mid-career professionals face. You've checked the boxes and climbed the ladder. You've kept pace with expectations. Yet one morning you wake up, and the spark is out of sight—if not completely gone. You're not sure where it went, what changed, or when. Or why the same routine now feels off. But it does.

You're still delivering. You're still respected. And yet inside, something is fogged over. You start second-guessing: Why does this feel heavy? Is it burnout or boredom? Is it time to move on or dig in?

This book is for that exact moment.

It's the moment between achievement and authenticity. The space between what was, what is, and what wants to be. It's the fog. And you're not alone in it.

When the Map No Longer Matches the Terrain

Most of us were handed a professional map early in life. Study hard. Climb steadily. Earn credentials. Lead teams. Collect promotions like merit badges. So what happens when the terrain changes?

The workforce has shifted. Industries are evolving overnight. AI is changing the world around us daily. The promise of loyalty from organizations has cracked. Even more, your own internal compass has shifted. What used to motivate you no longer does. This reality is not a flaw. It's *evidence of growth.*

You are not lost. You're just in unfamiliar territory that your old map doesn't account for. And, shocking as it may be, most mid-career professionals walk through this. They just don't always talk about it.

The Prestige, the Pressure, and the Fog: My Story

I know the fog well, because I lived in it.

After a successful run in recruiting, I was invited to pivot into internal audit consulting. A prestigious nationwide firm recruited me into their elite team, a group known for working with some of the most powerful Fortune 500 companies in the U.S.

On paper, it was a dream. I was collaborating with professionals I deeply respected, many of whom I had worked with previously. We called our clients the "billion-dollar babies," and the role gave me access to boardrooms, executive leaders, and projects that many would consider career-defining. It was glamorous. It was exciting. And it was everything I thought I wanted.

Until it wasn't.

After the glamour wore off, the *grind* settled in: long hours; cross-country flights; constant time zone shifts. It wasn't just the schedule. It was the *misalignment*.

Our firm uncovered serious financial discrepancies at some of the most respected publicly traded companies. For example, revenue leakage was so significant that it was like leaving a financial faucet running full blast into the abyss.

And yet, our clients could choose whether to act on our findings or ignore them entirely.

We weren't offering soft recommendations. We were surfacing measurable risks. And when multi-million-dollar issues were met with polite shrugs, I started feeling something I hadn't felt in years: a deep internal unease. I no longer believed in the impact of what I was doing. It became harder to look in the mirror at the end of a long day and say, "This matters."

When the company offered me a seven-year contract, something inside me paused. That wasn't just a job offer. It was a mirror. I had to ask myself: *Do I want seven more years of this version of me*? So, I turned to my "personal board," a circle of trusted advisors and peers who knew my experience, strengths, and my soul. I asked the tricky question: "*If not this, then what*?"

Through deep self-reflection, prayer, and honest conversations, I realized something fundamental: I had become disconnected from who I really was and what I stood for. I wanted my work to leave evidence of impact. I needed to realign.

And so, I made a pivotal move, not out of rebellion, but out of resolve. I walked away from prestige and back toward purpose. I reclaimed my truth. I chose to show up not just as a professional, but as a person aligned.

The Science of Misalignment

When your career no longer aligns with your values, energy, or identity, your body and brain know long

> **"When your career no longer aligns with your values, energy, or identity, your body and brain know long before your resume does."**

before your resume does. Professionals often dismiss the early signs of misalignment as stress or fatigue. Fog is not just about being overworked. It's about being disconnected from your purpose. It's the cost of what I call 'congruence erosion': the gap between what you value and what you do.

According to the American Psychological Association, chronic misalignment at work activates your body's stress response system, even when there's no urgent danger present. Cortisol rises, making it harder to focus. Dopamine drops, reducing your sense of motivation and joy. Decision fatigue sets in, making even small choices feel heavy.

Your brain is wired to crave meaning. When your role lacks it, you subconsciously enter "preserve energy" mode. You start avoiding hard conversations, dreading Monday meetings, and feeling perpetually behind. As Dr. Bessel van der Kolk reminds us, "The body keeps the score"—especially when your soul isn't being heard.

Gallup's State of the Global Workplace Report found that only 23% of employees are actively engaged at work. Disengagement isn't laziness. It's usually a mismatch between values and environment. The World Health Organization now includes burnout as an official occupational phenomenon, defined by emotional exhaustion, increased mental distance from one's job, and reduced professional efficacy.

And according to Harvard Business Review, mid-career is the most common time for professionals to feel disengaged, especially those in high-responsibility roles with few avenues for authentic expression or evolution.

You're not broken. You're misaligned. And that's something you can address.

The High-Achiever Fog Trap

Career fog is not just common among those who feel lost. It's surprisingly prevalent among high performers. In fact, the more ambitious, accomplished, and responsible you are, the more susceptible you may be. Why? Because high achievers are trained to push through, over-function, and suppress signs of discontent in the name of performance. They don't slow down. They double down.

Here's how it shows up:

- Staying in roles longer than is healthy because of loyalty, obligation, or sunk-cost thinking.
- Feeling guilty for "wanting more" when the title, salary, and perks look enviable.
- Avoiding reflection because it threatens to unravel a carefully constructed identity.

Many of my clients have built strong external brands, yet weak internal alignment. Their success outpaces their self-connection. They are seen but not centered. One executive client said it this way: "I've spent 26 years becoming who everyone else needed. Now I don't know who I am, or what I want."

The fog isn't failure. It's your success calling you deeper.

When Fog is Triggered by Trauma

Some career fog isn't gradual. It arrives suddenly, and with a crash. A layoff. A public failure. A toxic boss. A health scare. A restructuring that sidelines your team. These aren't just organizational changes. They're emotional events that hijack clarity and corrode confidence. If you've experienced a destabilizing event at work, your nervous system may still be in protection mode: Don't try again. Stay small. It's not worth it. Don't trust anyone.

This response is why psychological safety is essential to reimagining your career. You cannot dream forward when your system is locked in self-defense. If you've experienced workplace trauma, slow down. Before asking "What's next?" ask "What needs to heal?" Fog triggered by trauma doesn't clear with action. It clears with compassion.

"You cannot dream forward when your system is locked in self-defense."

From Autopilot to Aligned: Amanda's Story

Amanda was a 20-year veteran in the finance sector. She came into our coaching with this phrase: "I don't know who I am outside of my title." She had money, recognition, and success, yet no time for creativity, movement, or presence with her family. When we explored her core values, Amanda named Freedom, Vitality, and Authenticity as non-negotiable. None of them was currently present in her day-to-day life.

"I don't know who I am outside of my title."

Instead of quitting overnight, we developed a strategy. She used new tools to redesign how she led, delegated, and structured her calendar. Within 90 days, her team's performance improved significantly. Within a year, she made a career move to a purpose-driven fintech company where she's now thriving and mentoring future leaders.

Amanda didn't escape the fog. She walked through it.

After the Layoff: Sam's Story

Sam was a senior operations leader at a global logistics company. For 16 years, he had built his team, streamlined systems, and led with integrity. Then the email came: Restructure. Position eliminated. Effective immediately. He was stunned, and not just professionally. He unraveled.

"My whole identity was tied to that badge I wore every day," he told me. "Who am I without it?" In our first coaching session, Sam used words like "invisible," "disposable," and "unanchored." The fog he felt wasn't confusion. It was grief.

We didn't rush to resumes or LinkedIn updates. We paused. We created space for him to process what had happened and what it had meant to him. Slowly, Sam began to remember who he was *before* the title. He rediscovered who he truly was beneath the title, reclaiming an identity "I AM" with clarity.

Three months later, Sam didn't just land a new job. He rebuilt himself into a new version. One that no employer could take from him. Sam shared with me, "Losing that role was the best worst thing that ever happened to me. It forced me to stop outsourcing my worth."

A Personal Note

If you've made it this far into the chapter, pause and honor that. You've looked directly at something many professionals avoid: the truth of misalignment. You've named what's felt invisible: the restlessness, the doubt, the exhaustion, the ache for more.

Fog doesn't mean failure. It means your soul is too big to keep pretending. It means your story needs a rewrite. Not because you've messed up, but because you're ready for more.

Elevation Practice: Clearing the Fog

Take time this week to reflect on these questions. Write your answers in the D by D - Interactive Workbook or your personal journal.

1. **What signals of career fog have I experienced lately?** Consider emotional, physical, or professional signs. Be honest. Write without editing yourself.
2. **What stories am I telling myself about why I "can't" make a change right now?** Where might those stories be rooted in fear, fatigue, or old identity scripts?
3. **What do I deeply value that I'm not currently seeing evidence of in my career or life?**
4. **When was the last time I felt truly aligned, energized, or "in flow"?** What was I doing, and who was I being?
5. **Who can help me name the fog and begin navigating forward?** Think of mentors, peers, coaches, faith-based advisors, or your own "personal board."
6. **What's one small action I can take this week to move toward clarity?**

Next Chapter Preview

You've recognized the fog. Now it's time to understand what it's pointing you toward.

In Chapter 2, we'll explore The Professional Crossroads, that pivotal moment when you realize disruption isn't happening to you. It's happening for you.

Chapter 2

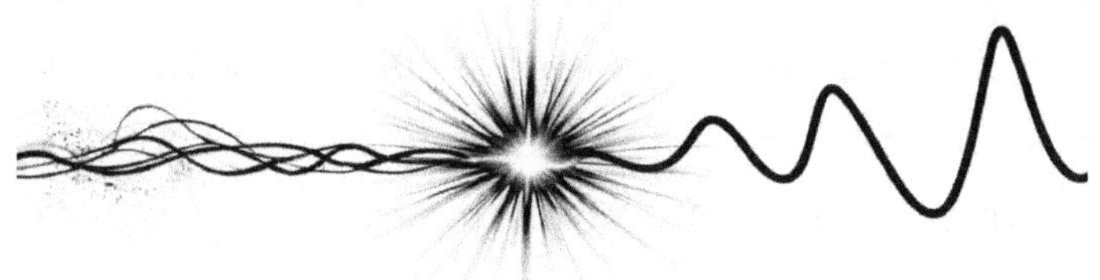

THE PROFESSIONAL CROSSROADS

"Midlife is when the universe gently places her hands upon your shoulders, pulls you close, and whispers in your ear: I'm not screwing around. All of this pretending and performing, these coping mechanisms that you've developed to protect yourself from feeling inadequate and getting hurt, has to go."

—Cheryl Strayed

The Pause That Changed Everything

It was an ordinary Tuesday, the kind that hums with a rhythm you've rehearsed for years. My phone glowed with back-to-back meetings. Emails cascaded in from clients in Seattle and new prospects in Scottsdale. From the outside, my life looked enviably successful: the founder of a respected executive-search and coaching firm, with a full roster and a reputation built on results.

And yet, in one small pocket of stillness between calls, I stopped. My hand hovered over the keyboard, and before I could stop myself, the question surfaced: "***Is this it?***"

That single thought, as quiet as a breath, required a response. It was not an emotional whim or fleeting dissatisfaction. It was a prompt that demanded an answer—a pull, a whisper, a deep stir telling me change was imminent. I didn't know what form it would take, however, I knew a shift was coming.

For weeks afterward, I tried to shake it off. I told myself it was fatigue, a natural ebb after years of growth. But that whisper kept coming back, louder each time, until it became impossible to ignore.

I have since learned that many professionals encounter this moment: a sudden realization that the path they've been climbing no longer inspires them. Some call it burnout, others a midlife crisis. I call it the **crossroads—a pivotal chance to reevaluate direction**.

What Happens at the Crossroads

The professional crossroads is deeply personal and often isolating. It's the moment when the path you've been on starts to blur, and the road ahead is uncertain. You've built, achieved, and contributed. Yet somewhere in the journey, your sense of self has dimmed.

For many professionals, disruption doesn't arrive like an earthquake. More often, it creeps in quietly. It's not always a layoff or a merger, though it certainly can be. Sometimes it's the unshakable fatigue in your bones, the resistance to opening your laptop, the quiet ache of knowing your work no longer reflects who you are becoming.

Other times, it's a corporate shakeup that turns your world upside down overnight.

From Valuable to Invisible: Mark's Story

Mark spent twenty-five years with the same global manufacturing company. He built teams, delivered results, and climbed the ladder one promotion at a time. From the outside, his career looked like the picture of stability.

Then one morning, he received a ten-minute calendar invite with HR and his regional vice president. Ten minutes later, it was over. The company was "restructuring." His position was eliminated. His twenty-five-year career ended before his coffee had gone cold.

When we spoke a few weeks later, he was still trying to make sense of it. "I felt like I'd been erased," he told me. "One day I was valuable. The next day I was invisible."

Mark wasn't just grieving a job. He was grieving an identity. He was at a crossroads.

For decades, his sense of worth had been tethered to a title, a team, and the rhythm of quarterly goals. When the title disappeared, it left a question many high achievers quietly fear: *Who am I if I'm not this role?*

This is the paradox of professional success. The more accomplished we become, the easier it is to mistake our position and title for our identity. The crossroads is where we must redefine our sense of value beyond roles.

Disruption has a strange gift, *it forces clarity.*

Over the next several weeks, Mark began to examine what had actually energized him throughout his career. It wasn't the reporting structure or the corporate ladder. It was the mentoring. The problem-solving. The moments when he helped younger leaders find their footing.

For the first time in decades, he wasn't asking, *What job can I get next?* He was asking a better question: *Where do I create the most value?*

That shift changed everything. Within a year, Mark transitioned into a leadership advisory role with a mid-sized firm undergoing rapid growth. Instead of managing the same operational cycle year after year, he was helping multiple leaders navigate the exact challenges he had spent decades mastering.

The layoff that once felt like erasure became a catalyst. Mark didn't just rebuild his career.

He redesigned it. And that is the essence of *Disruption by Design*: the moment when an unexpected ending becomes the doorway to a more intentional beginning.

For others, the crossroads arrives internally. You wake up one morning, look at your calendar, and feel an inexplicable resistance to everything on it. There's no external crisis. Just a growing sense of dissonance. It's not burnout. It's *awakening*.

> **"It's not burnout. It's awakening."**

According to Harvard Business Review, professionals between the ages of 40 and 55 experience the highest rate of mid-career stagnation, often driven by "achievement fatigue," the exhaustion that comes *not from failure* but from *success without meaning.* And in Deloitte's 2024 Human Capital Trends Report, nearly 70% of respondents said they were re-evaluating their relationship with work to better align with their personal values and purpose.

It's not that we're tired of working. We're tired of working without a *why*.

The Unseen Weight of High Achievers

High achievers often carry the heaviest burdens in silence. We're the ones others turn to for answers, for strategy, for vision. We're rewarded for our resilience but rarely invited to explore our restlessness. We've built strong reputations by pushing through discomfort, solving problems, and delivering results, even when our own souls were signaling the need for change.

I've coached executives who run billion-dollar divisions, founders who've exited their companies, and nonprofit leaders with life-changing missions. At some point, each one said the same thing: "I've done everything I was supposed to do... so why do I feel this way?"

Success is not a safeguard against disconnection. In fact, for many, it's the very pedestal that makes stepping off so terrifying. The truth is, continuing down a misaligned path simply because it looks impressive is one of the most expensive decisions you can make.

The higher we climb, the harder it becomes to admit we're unfulfilled. Admitting doubt can feel like risking credibility.

And yet, some of the most powerful breakthroughs I've witnessed began with a whisper of honesty: *I'm no longer the person I once was, and I no longer fit in these shoes.*

The Role of Curiosity in Crossroads

One of the most underutilized tools during career disruption is curiosity. Not curiosity about the next job title or company, but curiosity about oneself. When clients enter a transition space, I often ask, "What are you curious about that you've never given yourself time or permission to explore?"

This question alone opens floodgates. And sometimes those floodgates are tears, from the awareness that either nobody has ever asked, or that they weren't willing to even consider it.

One client, an operations executive, realized when I asked this question that she'd spent 18 years climbing a ladder she didn't even want to be on. Through our coaching, she rediscovered her love for education and launched a leadership academy for college students. It wasn't a pivot born of desperation; it was one born of permission. Curiosity became her compass.

Curiosity turns fear into wonder, inviting possibility. It makes disruption not only bearable, its also exciting, creative, and freeing.

The Myth of Linear Success

We've been taught to believe in linear success: go to school, get the job, climb the ladder, retire. For most of us, life doesn't unfold that way. Success is a spiral, not a straight line. It involves reinvention, recalibration, and yes, sometimes retreat.

Our society celebrates beginnings and endings, yet we don't talk enough about the middle, the messy, murky middle where clarity hasn't fully formed, and yet staying the same is no longer an option.

That middle space is where real transformation happens. It's where our deepest questions rise. It's where the voice of intuition gets louder. And it's where we must decide whether to default—or design.

Default Versus Designed Disruption

Disruption comes in two forms. Default disruption *happens to us*. Designed disruption *happens through us*.

> **"Default disruption happens to us. Designed disruption happens through us."**

Default disruption often feels like chaos. You're laid off. Your department gets reorganized. You lose your title, and with it, your identity. You feel unmoored, stripped of something you didn't realize had become so core to your sense of self.

Designed disruption begins when we stop resisting and start listening. It's when we take ownership of the pause and use it as a catalyst for clarity. We ask ourselves: "What is this moment trying to teach me?"

Transformation starts at the crossroads—when we reflect honestly on where we are and actively choose our next step instead of drifting by default.

From Cost-Cutting to Clarity: Laura's Story

Take Laura, a senior tech executive. After fifteen years at the same company, she was laid off in a round of cost-cutting. "I don't even know who I am without this title," she told me, her voice trembling through our first Zoom call.

Her confidence was shattered. Through our work together, Laura began to see the layoff as a release, an opportunity to rebuild on her terms. Within six months, she launched a consulting practice rooted in her passion for mentoring women in leadership. Within a year, she had doubled her previous income, had flexibility in her schedule to volunteer in her community, and rediscovered joy in her work and life.

Her identity wasn't lost; it was *waiting to be redefined*. As Simon Sinek reminds us, fulfillment doesn't come from standing still —it comes from living on purpose.

From Expertise to Essence

At the peak of our careers, we are often praised for our expertise. However, what many professionals begin to crave isn't just mastery; **it's meaning**. They want their work to feel like an extension of who they are, not just what they know.

Essence goes beyond competence. It asks: What part of you longs to be expressed in your work? What conversations light you up? What problems keep you thinking long after hours?

When you begin reconnecting with your essence, strategy follows. Your value proposition becomes clearer.

Your next step becomes more aligned—your confidence returns, not because of a title, instead because of truth.

The Sacred Pause

In a world obsessed with motion and metrics, stillness can feel like failure. Yet in truth, the pause is sacred. It's the threshold between who you've been and who you are becoming. As Stephen Covey memorably expressed, capturing the spirit of Viktor Frankl, "Between stimulus and response, there is a space. In that space is our power to choose our response."

When we rush transition, we risk repeating old patterns and missing insight. By pausing, we create space for wisdom, clarity, and genuine alignment. Honoring this pause is what enables us to consciously shape our next chapter, making our decisions intentional and true to ourselves.

One of my clients shared that she finally took a whole weekend away, no laptop, no planning, and it was in the silence of those two days that she wrote the outline of the nonprofit she would later launch. "I didn't realize how much clarity I'd been blocking by always being busy," she said. "The pause didn't just help me hear my calling. It reintroduced me to myself."

Another client, a VP of Sales, spent two months unemployed and called it the most enlightening time of his life. "At first, I panicked," he admitted. "But then I started hiking in the mornings, journaling in the afternoons. I had space to think, and for the first time in decades, I wasn't answering to anyone else's calendar but my own." He eventually accepted a role that paid less; however, it aligned deeply with his values. "I feel like I finally came home to myself."

Their stories aren't rare. This awareness is what happens when we decide to *design our disruption*.

The Identity Trap

One of the most significant challenges at this stage of life isn't external. It's internal. For high-performing professionals, identity becomes interwoven with performance. We are praised for productivity, not authenticity. We will explore this further in Chapter 5.

Mid-career professionals often find themselves in a friction between *what we do and who we are*. Our professional identity can become a mask we wear so convincingly that we forget there's a face beneath it.

I remember working with Nathan, a global sales leader whose job had defined him for nearly two decades. His voice carried both pride and fatigue when he told me, "My title has always opened doors. I'm afraid of who I'll be without it."

During our sessions, we conducted the Core Values Index (CVI) assessment and explored what had once drawn him to that work: the thrill of connection and the satisfaction of helping others succeed. Over time, he realized it wasn't the title that made him influential; it was his ability to build trust.

That insight freed him. Within a year, he transitioned into a role as a coach for emerging sales leaders, guiding them to find their own confidence. That's the shift that happens when you clarify identity. It's no longer about chasing validation; it's about leading from alignment.

We all face this mirror at some point, the one that reflects not our resume, but our *truth*. Who am I when the title fades? Who am I beyond the accolades? Who am I when I stop performing and start becoming?

As Adam Grant reminds us in *Think Again: The Power of Knowing What You Don't Know*, "When we define ourselves by our roles, we lose the ability to rethink ourselves when the world changes." That's why the crossroads feels so unsettling. It forces us to confront the question: Who am I without the role I play?

The truth is, you are more than your resume. You are more than your most recent success. You are a whole, evolving human being, capable of growth, reinvention, and purpose. As Brené Brown writes, "Owning our story and loving ourselves through that process is the bravest thing that we will ever do."

When professionals begin to reclaim their story, they also reclaim their power. And with that power, they begin to build again on purpose.

What Triggers the Crossroads?

Crossroads moments come in many forms. Sometimes they arrive like thunder, other times like a whisper. What unites them is the internal invitation to evolve.

- **Burnout:** The slow erosion of purpose beneath performance.
- **Layoffs or Reorganization:** The sudden removal of external structure.
- **Stagnation:** Realizing you've mastered your craft but lost your curiosity.
- **Identity Shifts:** Personal growth outpacing professional context.
- **Life Changes:** Empty nesting, relocation, divorce, or health events that realign priorities.

Each disruption carries pain, yet also potential. When we shift from asking *'Why is this happening to me?' to 'What is this making possible for me?'*, we enter the realm of **design**.

The Cost of Avoidance

Many professionals ignore the call to evolve until circumstances force their hand. The result? Prolonged disengagement, burnout, and even physical symptoms of stress. The American Psychological Association reports that **77% of workers regularly experience stress-related physical effects, and mid-career professionals rank among the highest risk groups**. Stress, when unacknowledged, becomes misalignment made visible.

Ignoring the crossroads doesn't delay the disruption. It magnifies it. The question is never *if* change will come, but *how* you will meet it.

The Courage to Redefine

Every transformation begins with permission: the permission to pause, to question, and to imagine something new. Jim Collins, in *Good to Great*, said, "The good is the enemy of the great." Many professionals get trapped in good. Good salary. Good title. Good benefits. However, good can quietly suffocate the extraordinary.

Courage, in this context, is not the absence of fear. It's the willingness to walk into uncertainty with curiosity. When you begin to view your disruption as a design opportunity, you reclaim authorship of your story.

Preparing for the Crossing

When I finally stopped resisting the question, *Is this it*?, I discovered it wasn't an accusation, it was an awakening. That question wasn't suggesting I had failed; it was inviting me to expand. It allows us to move from fear to faith, from exhaustion to energy, from uncertainty to clarity.

"Is this it? I discovered it wasn't an accusation, it was an awakening."

Every disruption carries within it an opportunity: the chance to realign who we are with what we do. However, that opportunity will pass us by if we don't recognize it. As you read this book, you'll be invited to pause and reflect, just as I did. To examine the choices that have shaped your path. To reintroduce yourself to the part of you that already knows what's next. Even if that knowing feels faint right now.

A Personal Note

If parts of this chapter felt uncomfortably familiar, that's not something to ignore. It's something to explore. Professional crossroads rarely appear when life is calm and predictable. They tend to arrive when something inside you begins to stir and you feel less comfortable on the path you've been following. That realization can feel unsettling, however it's also significant. Awareness is often the first signal that change is beginning to take shape.

This chapter is not just about reflection. It is about reclaiming your narrative. It is about letting go of outdated versions of yourself and welcoming the version that's always been waiting beneath the surface.

The exercise ahead is designed to help you slow down, reflect honestly, and begin naming the crossroads you may be standing in today. You don't need to know the entire plan. You only need to take the next right step.

Elevation Practice: The Pause Inventory

Before you move forward, pause here. Take an intentional inventory of where you are right now. Write your answers in the D by D - Interactive Workbook or your personal journal.

1. **What areas of my career or life currently feel out of alignment?**
2. **Where am I experiencing energy drain versus energy gain?**
3. **What parts of my identity or work no longer reflect who I am becoming?**
4. **What am I curious about that I haven't permitted myself to explore?**

Your Action Step: Set aside one uninterrupted hour this week. No email, no phone, no distractions. Sit with these questions and write. Not to solve. To see.

Next Chapter Preview

You've paused. You've taken inventory. You've honored the moment.

In Chapter 3, we'll explore how to move from reaction to intention, from drifting into disruption to consciously designing your next evolution. Because transformation doesn't begin when the plan is ready, it starts when you answer the call.

Chapter 3

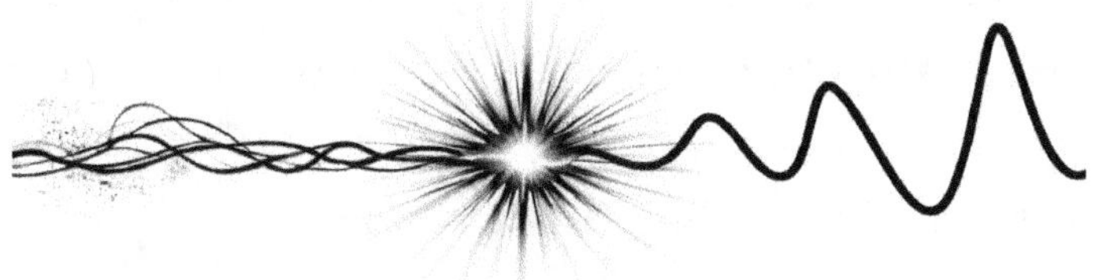

DISRUPTION BY DESIGN

"You can't stop the waves, but you can learn to surf."

—Jon Kabat-Zinn

The Illusion of Control

When disruption strikes, our instinct is to seek control. We scramble to regain a sense of certainty, scanning for the nearest next step, the fastest exit from discomfort. More often than not, our attempts to force resolution lead us down default paths, decisions rooted in fear, not design.

I remember working with a brilliant VP of Marketing who had been unexpectedly laid off after her company merged with a competitor. Within days, she was filling out job applications, reaching out to recruiters, and tweaking her resume. "I just need to get back on track," she said. However, when we paused to explore what "track" meant, she realized she was chasing the safety of familiarity rather than the future she actually wanted. She was reacting, not designing.

The truth is: disruption is not the end of your story. It's the beginning of your authorship. And control isn't about forcing outcomes. It's about choosing a response. The distinction is subtle but life changing.

Similarly to Jon Kabat-Zinn's quote above, in our coaching practice we often say: "You can't control the wave, but you can position your board." That's the heart of strategic surrender: allowing what is, while choosing what's next from a place of grounded clarity.

"You can't control the wave, but you can position your board."

Disruption puts pressure on the narrative you've built for your life. The story that once gave you security can begin to feel limiting or outdated. In that pressure is an opportunity, if you allow it, to evolve how you relate to identity, ambition, and alignment. Control is often a coping mechanism. Design, on the other hand, is a courageous act of co-creation.

This chapter is about shifting from panic to possibility. It's about asking more profound questions. Instead of defaulting to "What do I need to fix?" you begin to ask, "What is ready to grow?"

Crisis Versus Calling

There is a moment in every transition when the question shifts from "*What do I do next*?" to "*Who am I becoming*?"

That's the moment you stop surviving disruption and start designing through it.

Author William Bridges, in his groundbreaking work *Transitions*, explains that change is situational, however transition is psychological. Losing a job, ending a partnership, or pivoting careers are *changes*. The *transition* is the internal reckoning: the letting go, the neutral zone, and the *new beginning*. This middle space, messy, uncertain, nonlinear, is where designed disruption lives. It's the arena where you begin to choose how you respond, how you reframe, and what you build.

In *Think Again*, organizational psychologist Adam Grant writes, "The hallmark of wisdom is knowing when it's time to abandon some of your most treasured tools and some of the most cherished parts of your identity." This chapter is about that ***wisdom***. It's about consciously choosing curiosity over certainty, clarity over comfort.

What feels like a crisis may actually be a calling. The discomfort you're feeling could be the signal that your life is trying to evolve. You are being asked to respond not with urgency, yet instead with authorship.

I've seen this shift in seasoned professionals who lost their jobs due to acquisition or downsizing. While the surface emotion was panic or grief, underneath was often a deeper ache, a realization that their career had drifted from who they really are becoming. The event that felt like a crisis became the catalyst for reinvention. The calling had been whispering for years. The disruption finally made it loud enough to hear.

When the Calling Gets Loud: My Story

There was a season when my business was growing, my calendar was full, and my reputation was strong. However, beneath the surface, I felt misaligned. My work no longer lit me up the way it once did. I had reached the summit I'd been climbing for years, only to realize the view didn't align with the vision.

It was during a quiet early morning flight that I finally asked myself: What am I being called to create now? Not what would be "safe" or "smart" or "expected," but instead, what would be aligned. That question unraveled me in the best way. It ushered in the decision to rebuild my business around what I call soul-aligned strategy.

The disruption had been unfolding quietly all along. I simply hadn't slowed down enough to listen. When I finally did, I stopped reacting and started designing.

And here's what I know: your disruption may not come in a tidy package. It might look like restlessness. Like resentment. Like fatigue. Yet underneath, there's usually a call. And when you answer it, the path forward, while not always easy, becomes unmistakably yours.

Our truest next step is rarely the loudest. It's the one that resonates, even if it scares us.

Reactive Versus Intentional: The Two Paths of Change

Most professionals take the reactive route because it's fast, familiar, and socially validated. You get laid off? Update your resume. You burn out? Find a new role. You feel uninspired? Take a vacation.

Intentional transformation begins with reflection, not reaction.

Here's a simple yet powerful concept: Reactive change asks, "How do I fix this quickly?" Intentional change asks, "What is this disruption here to teach me?" When you pause to ask the second question, you create space for insight. You begin to notice the outdated narratives, the silent longings, and the misalignments you've ignored.

Satya Nadella's leadership at Microsoft is a powerful example of intentional transformation. When he became CEO in 2014, the company was stagnating. Instead of doubling down on legacy strategy, Nadella led with what he called a "growth mindset," focusing on empathy, curiosity, and innovation. He challenged every team to rethink, relearn, and redesign.

While Nadella's transformation was organizational, the same principal applies at the individual level. In his book *Hit Refresh*, Nadella wrote: "The key is not only to learn but to unlearn." That is the heart of *Disruption by Design*. It's about consciously choosing a new lens; one aligned with who you are becoming.

Intentional change isn't a singular decision; it's a practice. It means revisiting your values weekly. It means questioning where your "yes" is coming from. It means noticing when urgency is driving the bus and gently taking the wheel back. When you get intentional, your calendar changes. Your conversations shift. Your vision sharpens.

Because when you stop reacting, you *start remembering what matters.*

The Risk of Staying Safe

One of the most significant risks in times of disruption isn't failure. It's settling. It's the quiet resignation that convinces you to take the "next logical step" even when your heart says otherwise.

> **"One of the most significant risks in times of disruption isn't failure. It's settling."**

From Plateau to Expansion: George's Story

George was referred to me by a close colleague who was concerned. George had been visibly stagnating. On paper, he was a high-achieving executive in a thriving tech company, generating millions in revenue. But in person? He was checked out. His spark was gone. The once-bright energy that lit up boardrooms and company strategy sessions had dimmed to a flicker, and even the sound of his wife and daughter's voices, he admitted, felt like background noise. George was existing, not living.

Our initial conversations revealed a sobering truth: George hadn't designed his life in a long time. He had been reacting, not creating; drifting, not deciding. His calendar was full, however his soul was empty.

We began the *Disruption by Design* process by exploring his Core Values Index (CVI) and identifying his "I AM" pillars. As we walked through the reflection together, I watched his shoulders shift and his expression soften, as if a man was finally being seen. He began reclaiming permission to be who he truly was, not just the executive his company had molded him into.

When we reached the point of writing his new professional positioning statement, something unexpected surfaced. George paused and said, "I can't finish this. I don't think I want to keep doing what I've been doing."

That's when we hit the real gold.

Instead of pushing forward with business as usual, we zoomed out and examined what once made him come alive. He confessed he had loved photography, dabbling in art, and had even dreamed of doing improv comedy years ago. However, that version of himself had long since been buried under quarterly quotas and family obligations. As he put it: "That's not my life now. I'm a corporate executive. I don't have time for my fantasy life."

I didn't sugarcoat it. "George, what's the cost of continuing to deny the parts of you that bring you joy?" His eyes dropped. His voice cracked. He quietly admitted, "I'm disconnected from my wife. I'm barely present for my daughter. And my performance at work is suffering." So, we built a new plan. Step one: Improv class. And from there? George began to rise.

Week by week, he showed up differently—lighter, funnier, more grounded. He prepped for his debut night at the local Seattle improv like it was a TED Talk. And when he crushed it on stage, he couldn't stop grinning. That version of George was alive. The numbness was replaced by nervous excitement and authentic joy.

His family felt the difference, too. He was more connected at home, rebuilding bonds and showing up to sports games and dinner conversations with renewed presence. The man who had once been emotionally distant was now leading with heart. Eventually, we agreed: the grind of corporate life was no longer sustainable or desirable. The transformation had already taken root. He didn't want to go back into the cave.

George took a sabbatical, an opportunity offered by his employer, and used the time to rediscover his creative self. He entered photography competitions and won first place. He finally wrote the book he'd been putting off. He explored teaching as a new path.

By the end of that sabbatical, he wasn't the same man. His energy, his values, and his outlook had evolved. Together, we built a roadmap to support his next pivot: becoming a professor of photography and literary expression at the local university.

Now he stands on stages, not just to perform, but to share his story. His message to others is clear: "You don't have to stay stuck, stagnant, or unfulfilled. You can reimagine your future. You just need the courage to choose it, and the right guide to walk beside you."

Designing your disruption requires a pause. It invites you to challenge the assumption that faster is better, that busy is successful, and that comfort equals alignment. It asks: What does success look like *now, at this season, in this moment*, for the version of you that's emerging?

To stay "safe" often means to stay stuck. There is no growth without some measure of risk. But the risk of inauthenticity outweighs the risk of reinvention. When you settle, you silence your soul. When you design, you activate it.

Playing it safe often has a cost, and it's usually paid in missed potential. While fear whispers worst-case scenarios, your intuition is quietly pointing toward something greater. The question is: *what are you listening to*?

Anchoring in Meaning

When disruption shakes the ground beneath you, the most important thing you can do is reconnect with what matters most. That's your inner compass. And you access it by anchoring in meaning.

When you anchor in meaning, your decisions may feel bold to others, however, they will feel true to you. And that truth creates resilience. Meaning creates momentum. It transforms disruption from something to survive into something to steward. Meaning also roots you when the path feels foggy, or the road gets bumpy. Even your ideal path has challenges. With depth of meaning and clarity of alignment, you can move through those challenges with greater ease and more energy. You may not know every step; however, you'll see the direction. That is enough to begin.

The Power of the Pause

The pause isn't passive. It's active stillness. It's where clarity is born. Yet most professionals are conditioned to push through, to act quickly, to avoid the discomfort of not knowing. However, what if the pause is the portal? What if the space between what was and what's next holds the very insight you've been chasing?

In our process, we guide clients through what we call "strategic pausing." It's a short yet powerful framework: First, stop reacting. Second, scan your truth, what's real, not just rational. Third, seek alignment with what's calling you forward. This framework doesn't give you answers. It gives you access: to self-trust, to insight, to clarity. And that access is everything.

Some of the most transformative decisions I've witnessed didn't happen during a coaching session. They happened during a pause. A quiet walk. A weekend retreat. A journaling moment that turned into a breakthrough. Don't underestimate the space between the noise. Even five minutes of stillness can change the trajectory of your week. Make time for the pause. Build it into your calendar. Let it become a sacred space where your future self speaks.

The New Career Currency: Clarity + Courage

We're entering a professional era where certainty is obsolete, however clarity is invaluable. What organizations, clients, and

> **"Certainty is obsolete—clarity is invaluable."**

collaborators want most is someone who is anchored, authentic, and aligned.

The new career currency isn't just skill. It's clarity + courage.

Disruption by Design gives you both. It allows you to name what matters most, release what no longer fits, and align your voice, value, and vision. This framework isn't about making impulsive leaps. It's about strategic alignment. As Patrick Lencioni writes, "Success is not a matter of mastering subtle, sophisticated theory, however, rather of embracing common sense with uncommon levels of discipline and persistence."

Disruption by Design is that discipline. And it begins with the courage to ask: *What would I create if I weren't afraid of starting over*? This is the question that rewrites lives. This is the question that redesigns careers.

A Personal Note

For many professionals, life and career unfold through unconscious alignment, decisions are made from habit, expectation, or momentum. However, awareness changes everything.

Once you begin to recognize where your choices no longer reflect who you truly are, you gain the opportunity to shift from drifting to designing. Disruption, when approached with intention, is not chaos. It is design, and design begins in that moment of awareness. The exercise that follows will help you start identifying where your life is aligned, and where it may be calling for a more intentional direction.

This is your permission slip to stop defaulting. To start designing. You are not here to follow a path. You're here to make one. The real question isn't what will you do? It's who are you becoming? And the only person who can answer that is you.

Elevation Practice: Designed Disruption

Use the following questions to deepen your alignment with intentional disruption. Write your answers in the D by D - Interactive Workbook or your personal journal.

1. **Where am I currently reacting out of fear instead of choosing with intention?**
2. **What outdated narrative or assumption am I still carrying?**
3. **If I permitted myself to start over, what would I design?**
4. **Where do I feel most called right now, even if it doesn't make sense yet?**
5. **What would courage look like in this season?**
6. **What might I gain if I released the need for certainty?**
7. **In what ways is my current discomfort a signal of future growth?**
8. **What story do I want to tell one year from now about this moment?**

Write your answers with honesty. Don't worry about being "right." Focus on being real.

Next Chapter Preview

You've named the fog. You've identified the crossroads. You've felt the disruption. You're beginning to ask better questions.

In Chapter 4, we'll define ***clarity*** as more than vision. It's a disciplined process that builds unshakable confidence. When you anchor in this clarity, the fog lifts, and the brilliance within you becomes unmistakably visible.

The journey continues. However, this time, it's by design.

Chapter 4

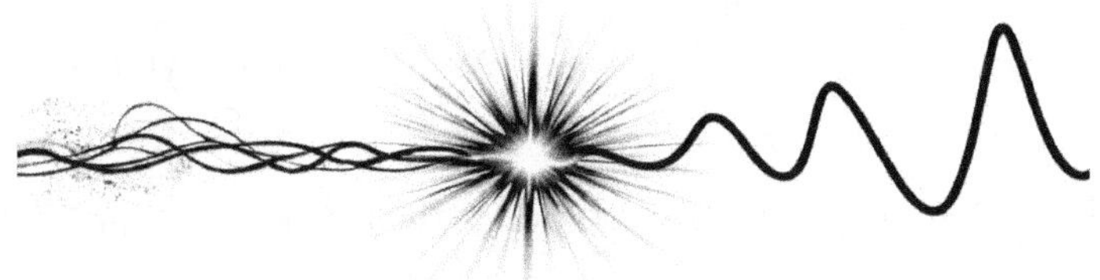

THE IMPORTANCE OF CLARITY

"Clarity affords focus."

— Thomas Leonard

Clarity is Not a Luxury, it's a Lifeline

In a world that constantly tells you who to be, what to do, and how to measure success, clarity is an act of defiance. It's the courage to ask: What do I actually want? Who am I, really? What fills my soul? Many of my clients grapple with this scenario, which is what leads them to me.

Clarity Stripped to Powerful Restoration: Donna's Story

A significant example of this came from my client Donna. She came to me as an overwhelmed executive working for one of the largest technology firms in the world. Her posture was defeated, as if she were carrying a significant weight on her shoulders. Her voice was quiet and unsure. No smile. The look of pain was a mask overshadowing the real person hidden inside.

Donna had been with the company for six years, earned three impressive promotions in that short period, and was currently leading IT launch readiness for their $19 billion Cloud and Enterprise organization. Clearly, she was seen as someone capable of leading a major launch.

Yet despite this visible promotion and worldwide launch, Donna felt defeated, undervalued, questioned her abilities, was depressed, and was unclear about her future. She felt feelings of unworthiness, a loss of energy, and a loss of drive. It was safe to say she was lost. A friend who had previously worked with me referred her, and we began identifying how she arrived at this place and whether I could help her find her way back.

Over the course of a month of regular meetings, we reached the first step in rebuilding her foundation: identifying her "I AM." Donna started emerging from the masks of defeat. She began entering our meetings with a huge smile, even a twinkle in her eye. Shoulders back, standing tall, a strong voice full of energy, cheer, and conviction, with excitement to take her career to the next level.

The Moment That Changed Everything

This was my coaching "ah-ha" moment. During this time, while working with Donna, I created a workshop to promote The Executives Agent™ coaching practice I had developed over the previous few years. I hired a professional to videotape the entire workshop for future marketing. I asked three clients to share their testimonies, and Donna was one of them.

We were on stage in a room of about 20 people, the video rolling as I introduced the three clients about to share their testimonies. I introduced Donna to the audience, and she said, "Before I share the successful outcomes of the program, first I have to share something."

She looked at me, then the audience, and stated, "This woman saved my life. When I came to her, I was so distraught that I was planning to end my life. And this woman saved my life by reminding me **who I am** and helping me find my 'I AM,' which turned around my life."

The room was very quiet. This moment was the first time I had heard this. While fighting back tears, I looked into the audience and saw Donna's husband looking back at me. He nodded in agreement that Donna was telling the truth. Donna chose to share this truth publicly because she wanted others to know they weren't alone. It is hard to articulate the massive rush of emotions I felt in that moment, both the intense thankfulness that I was part of such a life-affirming situation and the feeling of holding back a waterfall of emotion while trying to maintain composure for the audience and camera.

This was my "ah-ha" moment that has forever changed the way I approach working with clients.

After this experience, I realized something very deep, moving, humbling, and honest about this coaching work.

It is more than impacting just a career. This work impacts the entire human life and the lives of those with whom they interact. This reality was a far greater responsibility, requiring more reverence, compassion, humility, and care than I had realized.

A person's career is far more impactful than people think, until they find themselves without a job, set aside from the path they were on, or simply cut down to their core by a manager or colleague of influence. Without a foundation of clarity to provide confidence, they can lose all sense of what they are capable of achieving or how much worth they actually have. It is truly astonishing how much one person can shape another's beliefs about who they are and what they have to offer in this life.

Recognizing this was Donna's challenge. She had a very successful career until she encountered one person, a manager in her department, who was able to strip away her confidence, self-respect, and memory of her proven past successes.

After the workshop, her husband told me that he could not reach her where she had fallen. He was scared and felt helpless. Donna had gone from being completely connected to the truth of who she was to complete confusion and disconnection from that truth.

I will forever be thankful for the opportunity to work alongside Donna and help remind her who she is. Helping to lead her back to her true identity, seeing her come back to clarity and her "I AM," radiant with confidence and ownership of who she is, has been one of those gifts in life you couldn't have imagined. And when you receive it, you know your mission is far greater than you.

You can't build a meaningful life or career from confusion. You can only create from clarity.

Clarity isn't Certainty, it's Connection

There's a common myth that clarity means having all the answers. It doesn't. Clarity is connection to your core, to what you were created to do and be, and to how your influence matters in the world. It's the difference between walking through fog and walking with purpose, even if the full path isn't visible.

As Marie Forleo says, "With clarity comes the courage to take bold action." We often seek confidence from outside, through credentials, reassurance, or accomplishments. Yet the most sustainable form of confidence begins with inner clarity. When you are deeply aware of who you are, your values, vision, and purpose, confidence is no longer something you perform. It becomes a natural state of being.

What Gets in the Way of Clarity

External Noise. We are bombarded with success metrics that have nothing to do with personal fulfillment: titles, money, social status, even likes and comments.

Internal Scripts. These are the "shoulds" you've internalized, often without question. You should want stability. You should be more successful. You should be grateful. You should stick with what works and is safe. The list goes on.

Fear of Change. Clarity demands truth. And sometimes that truth reveals a need for significant change. It's easier, in the short term, to stay confused than to risk the consequences of knowing.

As Tony Robbins puts it, "The truth will set you free, but first it will piss you off."

Why Mid-Career Clarity is Crucial

Mid-career is often painted as a time for consolidation. It is a time to reap from the *wisdom and experience* humans have gathered throughout their lives and careers. However, for many, it's when specific questions get louder: Is this all there is? Am I living the life I chose, or the one that was chosen for me? If I'm successful, why don't I feel fulfilled?

"Am I living the life I chose, or the one that was chosen for me?"

These are not signs of failure. They're invitations to clarity.

The Real Challenge isn't Burnout, it's Misalignment

Burnout gets all the attention. However, is that really what's happening? Let's look at what some experts say.

Recent research from Psychology Today emphasizes that long-term burnout often stems from a loss of meaning or purpose, and that reconnecting with deeper values can protect against true burnout. Dr. Steven Stonsney states, "Without meaning and purpose, burnout is inevitable, at work or in relationships."

The American Psychiatric Association, recently reported, that low self-awareness is linked to a 25% higher risk of burnout. People who lack insight into their own emotions, habits, or abilities are notably more vulnerable.

A study from Concordia University found that uncertainty at work, such as role ambiguity and a lack of leadership vision, correlates strongly with burnout, even more strongly than workload or complexity. Clear goals and purpose help combat this.

What if what you are feeling isn't exhaustion from work? What if it's actually the weight of living out someone else's ideal of a successful life? The ideas of what you are "supposed to" do, who you were "supposed to" become, and the expectations of what your parents or boss thought would be good for you?

I call this the hidden crisis of misalignment. It's the quiet internal conflict that occurs when the identity you show to the world no longer matches who you are inside. You can feel it most intensely in mid-career, when you're far enough along to have built a life, but not so far that you can't pivot.

What You Were Taught Versus Who You Are

From an early age, most of us are trained to perform. Perform for approval, for advancement, for safety. You learn to adapt.

I remember stepping into the business world for the first time at a prestigious firm in downtown Seattle. The dress code was no joke: full suits, every single day. For the men, that meant three-piece suits, expensive ties, gold cuff links, and shoes shined so bright you could see your reflection. For the women, it was tailored skirt suits with matching jackets, hosiery (yes, required), perfectly polished heels, and handbags that tied the whole look together.

It's almost hard to believe now, in a time when sneakers and smart casual dominate most offices. However, it raises an interesting question: did this strict dress code let people express who they really were, or did it mold them into the identity the business environment expected? Were they showing up as their authentic selves, or simply playing the part until they had enough influence to write their own rules?

Nearly everyone finds themselves molding into what the world will reward. But after a decade or two of performing the version of us that feels safe, the act starts to fracture. A crack appears, sometimes a quiet one, sometimes a canyon, and through it, truth begins to rise, uninvited but undeniable.

> **"Truth begins to rise, uninvited but undeniable."**

You start craving alignment with your inner core. You don't want to chase the next promotion if it means abandoning your sense of purpose. You want to ***know who you are*** and build a career and life that reflects that truth.

Clarify Your Why

Deep reflection, whether through journaling, values inventories, or meaning-focused coaching, is the practice of locating what I call your *solid foundation*. When life feels uncertain, this inner anchor helps you build on something firm. It enables you to uncover what truly matters, absorb stress, and overcome challenges.

Your "**why**" is your compass. When things get hard, and they will, it provides a sense of purpose, energy, resilience, and drive to press forward. Imagine facing adversity not with hesitation, yet with the ability to look it straight in the eye and smile.

Clarity of purpose transforms obstacles into stepping-stones. Instead of draining you, challenges can actually renew your energy, refine your purpose, and ignite your abilities as you recall exactly why you are pushing forward.

The Mountain Climber's Why

Think of a mountain climber on the final push to a summit. The air is thin, every breath burns, and the body pleads to stop.

However, the climber's why keeps them moving. Maybe it is the promise made to a loved one, the memory of past failure they refuse to repeat, or the dream that began as a child staring at that peak from a distance. Their why becomes oxygen when the air is thin.

Step by step, they climb, not because the mountain is easy, but because ***their why*** *is stronger* than their exhaustion. When they finally stand on the summit, looking out at the endless horizon, the view is not just a reward for endurance. It is a reminder that *clarity of purpose* carried them upward when their bodies alone could not.

"Their why is stronger than their exhaustion."

In life, just like on the mountain, we reach our summits not because conditions are perfect but because our why anchors us when every part of us wants to give up.

Self-Efficacy + Purpose = Resilience

When people believe in their own abilities and pair that belief with a clear sense of purpose, resilience is the natural outcome. Self-efficacy is the conviction that "I can handle this," which fuels confidence and empowers action even in uncertain or high-pressure situations. Purpose provides the reason to act in the first place. Together, they create a powerful equation: *the mental strength to continue and the reason* ***why it matters***.

Consider the difference between someone who is simply capable and someone who is *capable and anchored in purpose, with a mindset of achievement*. The first may endure for a while, however, risks exhaustion when challenges stack up. The second draws on an internal reservoir of energy, a mindset replenished by their *why*. This differentiator is why research consistently shows that people with strong self-efficacy and purpose are far less likely to quit in the face of adversity. They view obstacles not as stop signs yet as proving grounds. In this way, resilience becomes more than survival; it becomes a source of growth, strength, and ***renewed clarity.***

Unwavering Resilience: Howard Schultz

Take the story of Howard Schultz, the visionary behind Starbucks. Schultz grew up in a working-class family in Brooklyn, where he saw firsthand the toll of financial struggle after his father lost his job due to injury. That early experience became his purpose: to build a company where employees would be treated with dignity and given benefits many corporations withheld.

When Schultz sought to expand Starbucks in its early years, he faced repeated rejection from investors. More than 200 people turned him down. His own attorney advised him against his goal. Many entrepreneurs would have walked away. However, Schultz's unwavering belief in his ability to lead, coupled with his deeply personal mission, kept him moving forward.

Today, Starbucks is a global brand, yet more importantly, it reflects the purpose that fueled its resilience: creating not just a coffee company, but a community built on respect.

Schultz's journey illustrates that when self-efficacy, the belief "I can do this," is paired with a *compelling why*, "this matters to me because...," setbacks lose their power to derail momentum. Instead, they become steppingstones toward greater strength and achievement.

At this stage, you've collected enough life experience to recognize what no longer fits, and there is enough time left to do something about it.

A Personal Note

You may not know precisely what your next job or move looks like. However, you can know whether it aligns with your values and your energy. Clarity isn't something you wait for. It's something you choose. And when you choose it, your direction, your voice, your next move stops being a question and starts becoming a design.

Elevation Practice: Clarity Reflection

Now is your moment to push aside the "should do" thoughts and let yourself identify what clarity means to you. Get really honest with yourself. Write your answers in the D by D - Interactive Workbook or your personal journal.

1. **What does clarity mean to you personally?** When in your life did you feel most clear? Where are things foggy or uncertain?
2. **Describe a time when gaining clarity gave you the confidence to take bold action.** What shifted inside you when the path became clear?
3. **What areas of your life would benefit most from greater clarity right now?** Consider relationships, career, purpose, health, or identity.
4. **What practices help you find clarity when you feel lost or overwhelmed?** Are there habits, rituals, or environments that reconnect you with your inner compass?
5. **If you had complete clarity about who you are and what you want, what might you do differently tomorrow?**

Next Chapter Preview

The core of clarity is identity. Until you know who you are, everything else is negotiation.

In Chapter 5, we'll dive deeper into the core of reinvention: identity. We will explore how your "I AM" drives every decision you make, every risk you take, and every outcome you create. It's time to get congruent, to align your inner truth with your external impact. We will move into the powerful process of unlearning and self-inquiry that leads you to your own personal clarity statement: your "**I AM**."

The journey continues. However, this time, it's by design.

Chapter 5

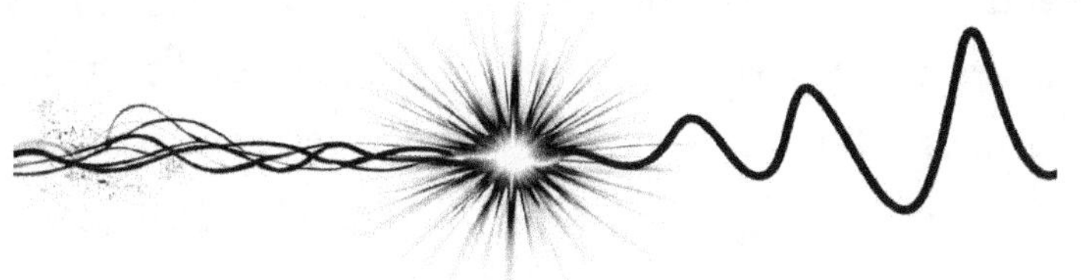

THE POWER OF "I AM" IN YOUR CAREER

"Who is it that can tell me who I am?

—William Shakespeare

The Moment You Realize You've Outgrown the Mask

At some point in your career, you'll walk into a meeting, a Zoom room, or a conference hallway and feel like a stranger to yourself. You'll hear your voice say all the right things, the polished and rehearsed things, and still feel something underneath isn't quite right. The spark is gone, or the alignment has shifted. You've followed all the rules, delivered all the results, and yet...

You can feel your inner self tugging at the edges.

That's not a breakdown. It's a breakthrough trying to begin. A career isn't just what you do. It's a container for *who you are becomin*g. When that "who" evolves, your old career identity starts to crack, not to punish you, but to promote you. In this chapter, we'll explore one of the most powerful forces shaping your career: the story you tell yourself when you say "I AM."

"A career isn't just what you do. It's a container for who you are becoming."

The Identity Behind the Resume

Ask someone, "Who are you?" and they'll almost always respond with what they do. "I'm a Marketing Director." "I'm a CEO." "I'm the VP of Sales." "I'm an Operations leader at a startup."

However, those are functions, **not identities**. And as roles evolve, especially in mid-career, professionals often experience disorientation. Layoffs, re-orgs, toxic cultures, acquisitions, AI, or quiet burnout can shake the foundation of who they thought they were.

According to research by the Harvard Business Review, professionals who strongly identify with their job titles report greater identity loss during career transitions, particularly in midlife. We don't realize how much of our "I AM" gets entangled with external validation. Titles. Promotions. Proving our worth and performing instead of being.

And then comes the whisper: "**I don't know who I am anymore, or who I want to be**."

The Perfection Persona: My Story

For years, my "I AM" was built on performance. I was the person who delivered early, exceeded expectations, and created calm in chaos. I was always "on," always composed, always carrying someone else's deadline like it was my own mission.

It worked...for a while.

However, over time, I noticed the cracks. I was exhausted. I was successful yet unfulfilled, and my tank felt empty more often than full. I knew I was serving and performing as expected. Yet I couldn't keep outrunning the feeling that I was wearing a version of myself that was becoming unsustainable and out of alignment with my passion and soul.

I remember the moment it changed. I was speaking to a client, listening to her describe how trapped she felt in a role that no longer aligned, and I realized: I was coaching her through the exact storm I was avoiding in myself.

It's truly remarkable how we can coach others or provide guidance that is clear, positively impactful, and results-oriented, helping others achieve outstanding accomplishments. Yet when the finger points at us, we cannot hear our own voice.

That's when I began doing the real work of redesigning my identity. I started reframing my "I AM" statements. I let go of the identity that served a past season. A friend whispered, "You don't have to do that anymore. You own your future." At that moment, I felt a release valve open and stepped into a more authentic presence as a coach, guide, leader, speaker, and not just a performer.

That shift wasn't just personal. It was spiritual. It was professional. And it was freeing.

The Psychology of Professional Identity

In *Working Identity: Unconventional Strategies for Reinventing Your Career*, Herminia Ibarra writes: "We are not one true self. We are many selves, and these selves emerge and develop over time." This is liberating and challenging. Most professionals believe that identity is fixed: that once you "become" something, it's forever. And the truth is, identity is a verb. It's a lived, evolving expression of your values, voice, and vision.

When your external work no longer aligns with your internal truth, tension arises. That misalignment causes stress, confusion, even anxiety, not because something is wrong, but because something wants to evolve.

When Identity Becomes a Mask

In high-achieving careers, we don't just build resumes. We build masks. These masks often begin as protective tools. We wear them to feel seen, safe, or successful. And over time, they become welded to our identity, and we forget they were ever optional.

You've probably met these masks in yourself or others: The "Fixer" mask, always available, always solving. The "Performer" mask never rests, never reveals weakness. The "Provider" mask takes care of everyone, even at your own expense. The "Expert" mask, be right, be certain, never say "I don't know." The "Pleaser" mask earns approval by being agreeable, adaptable, and invisible. The "Achiever" mask consistently achieves the highest rank on charts, goals, and contests. Workplaces reward these mask identities until they begin to suffocate the person underneath.

The Year I Took Off the Mask: My Story

In May 2011, I walked into a weekend workshop hosted by my church. The facilitators were authors, yet beyond that, I had no idea what to expect. The title alone caught my attention: "TrueFaced: Taking Off the Masks, Trusting God and Others with Who You Really Are." I remember thinking, I trust God, and I want to trust others with who I really am, so I'm in.

At that point, my life was full. I had endured a long, emotionally and financially exhausting divorce, then was fortunate to meet and marry the man of my dreams (Peter), was raising my three kids, and was managing a thriving career. On paper, everything looked golden. I was leading teams, managing complex client projects, active and serving in my church, chairing a professional women's group at a prestigious club, and showing up as the calm, poised, strategic, and highly capable leader in every room.

However, inside? I was tired. Not just from the pace of life, but from maintaining an identity I'd been performing for too long.

I was doing precisely what TrueFaced describes as "managing my image." I wore many masks: the ever-capable leader, the one who never needed help, never asked questions, always solving for everyone else, and never stopping long enough to ask what I actually needed.

That spring, I sat across from a trusted leader and mentor and finally admitted, "I don't know who I am without the doing." He looked at me gently and said, "Tina, you are enough. You don't need to perform perfectly all the time. You are enough, just as you are." That conversation cracked something open in me. Through that opening came grace, the quiet, steady voice of God, not condemning, yet instead, inviting.

That was the moment the transformation began. I started peeling back the layers of performance. I got honest about my limits. I let go of the need to impress and started practicing what it meant to be true, my true identity. It wasn't clean or easy. Transformation rarely is. It required trust, surrender, humility, and the courage to unlearn. And that was the year I began leading from *identity, not image*, and that changed everything.

The High-Performer Behind the Mask: Karen's Story

Karen was a former COO of a fast-scaling startup. Brilliant. Visionary. Respected. However, when her company was acquired, she was pushed out in a restructuring. Within three weeks, her calendar was empty, and her identity was shaken.

In our coaching session, I asked her who she believed she was now. She said, "I don't know. I used to be someone."

We explored what it meant and what it didn't. Slowly, we unpacked the mask she had worn: "I AM the one who keeps the machine running." It had made her successful.

It had also made her tired, detached, and unsure of what she truly wanted, or who she was.

Over three months, we reframed that mask. We created space for a new declaration using what I call the 3 Pillars of "I AM." She boldly claimed: "Vision Promoter / Value Clarifier / Relationship Advocate, who builds healthy systems, and that includes for myself." Today, she is a leader in a new geography, in a business that centers on values-first leadership. Her work is just as impressive. And now, so is her energy.

The Three-Stage Process: Removing the Mask

Here's the framework I share with clients and will guide you through now:

1. **Name the Mask.** What persona have you worn to stay safe or get approval? What did it protect you from? Common masks include the Pleaser, the Expert, the Savior, and the Chameleon.
2. **Notice the Cost.** What has this identity cost you emotionally, physically, relationally, spiritually? What parts of you got pushed underground to maintain it?
3. **Choose the True Self.** What do you know to be true about yourself now, even if it's still emerging? Can you begin to say, "I AM... enough / wise / evolving / valuable / creative / called"?

This work isn't theoretical. It's transformative. When you drop your masks, your voice strengthens. Your vision sharpens. Your values take the lead. Your "I AM" ignites your confidence, value, conviction, and clarity.

Why "I AM" is So Powerful: The Neuroscience

The words "I AM" are not just affirmations. They're **neural commitments**. When you repeat a belief about yourself, positive or negative, your brain starts to filter information to make it true. This pattern is called **confirmation bias**, and it's a survival function. Your subconscious is constantly scanning to match your self-declared identity.

"The words 'I AM' are not just affirmations. They're neural commitments."

Say "I AM terrible at change," and your brain will skip past opportunities for growth. Say "I AM adaptable and resilient," and your brain starts noticing how you've done that before.

Identity-based thinking can influence the brain's emotional circuitry. As psychiatrist Norman Doidge notes, repeated mental activity strengthens neural pathways, meaning that what we consistently think can gradually shape how we feel and respond to the world.

The more you repeat a thought with emotional charge, the more it becomes embedded. That's why so many professionals feel stuck. They aren't just blocked by their circumstances; they're being run by outdated identity scripts. As Hebb's Law states: "Neurons that fire together, wire together." When you change your "I AM," you change your inner programming.

Tool: The Career Identity Timeline

One of the most effective exercises I use with coaching clients is the Career Identity Timeline. Here's how it works:

Step 1: Map your career in 4-6 stages. Break it into meaningful chapters by role, company, or season of life. Example: Chapter 1: Hustler/Prover (early 20s). Chapter 2: Strategic Operator (late 20s). Chapter 3: Trusted Builder (mid-30s). Chapter 4: Burned Out Fixer (acquisition era). Chapter 5: Emerging Guide (pivot into consulting).
Step 2: Write your "I AM" belief in each stage. Ask: "What did I believe about myself during that time?" It might look like: "I AM only as good as my output." "I AM invisible unless I overdeliver." "I AM capable of leading with peace, not pressure."
Step 3: Circle the ones that still feel true and underline the ones you're ready to release.

This exercise is not just introspective; it's clarifying. You'll start to see what core beliefs are shaping your career behavior today and which ones need to evolve.

The Identity Upgrade After a VC Buyout: Marcus's Story

Marcus had been VP of Strategy at a high-tech firm for five years. When a prominent VC acquired the company, they brought in new leadership, and Marcus found himself suddenly redundant. He didn't see it coming. For months afterward, he felt paralyzed, not because he lacked opportunity, but because he no longer trusted his value.

In coaching, we traced his identity timeline. His "I AM" belief had subtly become: "I AM useful until I'm not." No wonder he wasn't excited to reenter the market. Through reflection and affirmation work, he reframed that to: "I AM an *Energizing Executive / Holistic Strategist / Business Solutions Optimizer*, who builds systems and solutions creating value beyond org charts."

That shift wasn't just semantic; it rewired his sense of authority. Within six weeks, he secured a fractional leadership role, which also allowed him to launch an industry roundtable series. He was no longer outsourcing his identity to a title.

Congruence: The Leadership Advantage No One Teaches

Congruence is when your inner world and your outer expression match. In leadership, it's the moment people stop following your title and start trusting your presence. It's not about being perfect. It's about being **true**.

"It's not about being perfect. It's about being true."

When leaders operate with a fractured identity, trying to be all things to all people, it leads to burnout, erosion of trust, performance masking, cultural confusion across teams, and disappointment that cuts to the core. However, when leaders show up as themselves, even when that self is evolving, it creates psychological safety, clarity, and connection.

Brené Brown on Authentic Leadership

In *Dare to Lead*, Brené Brown explains that vulnerability isn't weakness; it's courage in action. Mid-career professionals often think they must earn their place through composure, polish, or proving. Instead, research shows the opposite: authenticity drives connection and performance.

She writes: "People are sick of being with people who are 'everything to everyone.' We crave what is real. We follow people who show us themselves." That includes saying: "I'm still figuring this part out." "I made a mistake, and here's what I learned." "I'm not sure, but I trust us to find it together." These aren't admissions of incompetence. They're declarations of trust.

The Tech Exec Who Chose Real Over Right: Brandon's Story

Brandon was a VP of Product at a scaling SaaS company. Brilliant Innovator. Strategist. Leader. He was also exhausted. For years, he'd led with a hyper-polished, hyper-controlled energy that made him feel safe and made his team feel distant.

During a coaching series, we unpacked his mask: "I AM the guy who always knows." Yet inside? He was in a spiral of imposter syndrome. Together, we built a new narrative: "I AM a *Strategic Innovator / Collaborative Champion / Purpose-Driven Leader* who delivers innovative programs that exceed expectations while providing the best customer experience."

The shift wasn't dramatic at first. Brandon just started showing up a little more human. He admitted when a roadmap needed revision. He asked his team what they saw. He created a safe environment and inspired others to speak up.

One year later, he was leading a team at one of the world's largest identity technology firms, with employees following his lead, asking to be on his team, and mentoring others to success beyond their dreams. What changed? He stopped performing and started being.

A Personal Note

Imagine walking into your next season with this belief: "I AM aligned. I AM enough. I AM becoming." When you speak those words from a place of internal ownership, everything changes: your interviews, your client calls, your team meetings, your calendar, your peace.

Yes, it takes practice. And yes, you'll want to reach for the mask again some days. However, the more you return to the truth, the more that truth becomes your baseline.

Elevation Practice: "I AM" Reflection

This reflection helps you internalize the work we've just done. Find a quiet moment, no screen, no distractions, and answer honestly. Write your answers in the D by D - Interactive Workbook or your personal journal.

1. **What "I AM" statement has been driving your behavior, consciously or unconsciously?** (e.g., "I AM only valuable if I perform" / "I AM replaceable" / "I AM the fixer")
2. **Where did this belief originate?** What experience or system first reinforced it?
3. **What has it cost you to hold that identity?** Consider your time, relationships, peace, health, or creativity.
4. **What deeper truth is emerging in you now?** (e.g., "I AM already enough" / "I AM capable of change" / "I AM allowed to lead differently")
5. **What mask are you ready to set down permanently?** Describe it. Name it. Thank it. Then let it go.
6. **Complete this new declaration, out loud if possible:** "I AM ____________, and I give myself permission to grow."

Next Chapter Preview

Section 2: CLAIM

You have now gone through a very significant process, reframing your identity and likely experiencing a significant transformation. This experience is one of the most critical steps in your career and life.

Congratulations! Take a breath. Bask in the glow of who you have now identified with. Now let's use this renewed energy to embark on "Claiming" this new identity and create a clear direction to your future.

Section Two: Claim

OWN YOUR STRENGTHS, YOUR DIRECTION, AND YOUR NEXT MOVE

Chapter 6

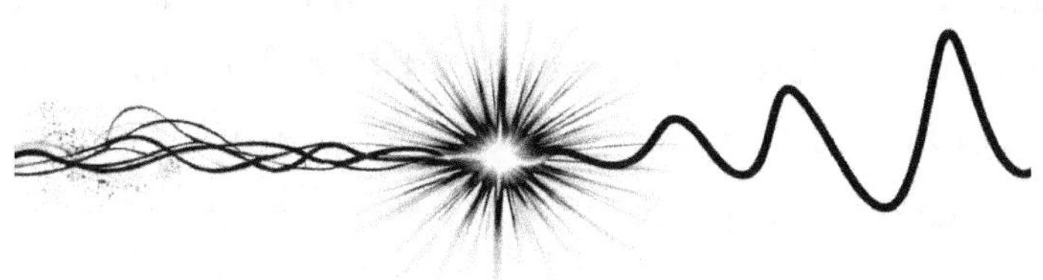

YOUR CAREER STORY, REWRITTEN

"You either walk inside your story and own it, or you stand outside your story and hustle for your worthiness."

— Brené Brown

You Are the Author

There is a sacred moment that arrives unannounced. It doesn't come in a spotlight moment, a big win, or a LinkedIn headline. It comes in the silence that follows, in the in-between. It sounds more like a whisper than a shout: "Is this really who I'm meant to be?" If you've ever asked that question, even quietly, you're not alone. That moment is a spiritual interruption. Not a breakdown, but a **breakthrough**.

For high-achieving professionals, the tension often emerges between *external success* and *internal congruence.* You've followed the rules, scaled the ladder, checked the boxes. However, somewhere along the way, the story you've been living no longer feels true. It may not be wrong, yet it's incomplete. You are not just a product of your resume. You are not defined by what others saw in you twenty years ago. You are not bound to a version of yourself that has expired.

You are the author. You hold the pen. And the story is yours to rewrite.

Story is Power

The story we tell ourselves about ourselves forms the foundation of our identity—the invisible scaffolding holding everything in place. More than skills, degrees, or achievements, narrative shapes our life's architecture. You are living inside such a story right now. It shapes what you reach for, what you tolerate, how you interpret failure, how you achieve success, and whether you believe reinvention is possible. This isn't just philosophy; it's science.

Dr. Dan McAdams, one of the leading voices in *narrative identity* at Northwestern University, discovered that **people who construct empowering and redemptive life stories** tend to live with *greater purpose, resilience, and satisfaction*, regardless of circumstances. He describes identity as a "constantly evolving narrative that integrates the reconstructed past and the imagined future into a coherent whole." In other words, you are not a fixed title. You are not a list of roles. You are the narrator of your evolution. And here's the good news: **narrators can change the plot**.

The Inherited Script

Most of us don't start as narrators. We begin as actors in someone else's play. Before we know who we are, we're told who we should be: "You're the responsible one." "You're the high achiever." "You're not the creative type." "You're not leadership material." "You're good with people, not strategy."

These early labels become our career scaffolding. Unconsciously, we write a script from expectations, praise, fear, and repeated success patterns. We wear these identities so long they feel permanent—but they're not. They're simply *unexamined scripts ready for review.*

The Interview That Changed Everything: My Story

The first major rewrite of my career story happened when I was least expecting it. At the time, I was an accountant on a traditional path, steadily progressing toward becoming a CFO. I worked for a small company that genuinely felt like family. It was safe, warm, and predictable. I cared about the people, and they cared about me.

Then one afternoon, I received a call that shifted everything. It was a recruiter from Robert Half International, a global powerhouse I knew of yet knew nothing about. I wasn't looking. I wasn't restless. I certainly wasn't thinking about recruiting as a profession. However, something nudged me to take the meeting. That decision led to four interviews. The second one, however, is the moment that changed everything.

I remember walking into one of Seattle's iconic high-rise towers and stepping into an office that felt like another world: polished glass, skyline views, and across the table, a Vice President named Ken dressed in a sharp three-piece suit, gold cufflinks, and personifying the kind of confidence that could silence a room. He was impressive, intimidating, and very clearly evaluating me.

During the conversation, he asked a question that caught me completely off guard: "Tell me about a time at work when you felt energy... maybe even fun. A moment that didn't feel like a job." I froze. The first honest answer that surfaced felt embarrassingly out of place in that elite corporate environment.

After a breath, I admitted, "Well... I used to work evenings and weekends at a restaurant. And even though it was a second job, I actually loved it. I had regular customers who would ask to sit in my section. It felt natural... effortless. I had fun." Then I immediately backtracked: "I probably shouldn't have said that. It has nothing to do with a role like this."

Ken leaned forward, smiling like he had just uncovered a hidden treasure. "Tina," he said, "that is *exactly why* I'm most interested in you." He went on: "People return to restaurants with mediocre food and great service, but not the other way around. What you just described is hard to teach. You have something we can't manufacture. Connection. Presence. The ability to make people feel seen. That's why you belong here, not because of a resume, but because of **who you are**."

Then he said the words that became a turning point in my life: "You should claim who you are, not hide from it."

That was the first rewrite of my story: from Accountant to Headhunter; from small family business to global corporation; from safety to stretched; from predictable to purposeful.

The Second Rewrite

And then came the second rewrite—the next turning point that reshaped everything in my professional journey. In May of 2024, I received another calling. This time it wasn't a phone call; it was a whisper in my spirit. A message so clear it felt like the kind of statement a parent makes when they're not asking... they're telling.

"You're playing too small. You cannot keep hiding the gifts I've given you. It's time to expand."

Regardless of your beliefs, you've possibly also experienced a moment that felt guided, unmistakable, unshakable. This was mine. I spent the following months diving deep, reflecting on the work I had done, the transformations I had facilitated, and the impact I had witnessed in the lives of the leaders I coached. I engaged in honest conversations with my husband, Peter, about who I was becoming.

What emerged was crystal-clear alignment: I needed to redesign my entire business around the identity I had grown into and finally finish the book I had started in 2015. I didn't need to "throw out" my past. I needed to reframe it: not small, but expansive; not a supporter, but a leader; not hidden, but called. This was not the end of a chapter. It was the beginning of a new story; written by the woman *I had finally become.*

From "Stuck" to Personal Brand: Nacho's Story

He sat across from me, polished and poised, with a resume and full company history meticulously prepared. His credentials were beyond impressive: UAM (Universidad Autónoma Metropolitana) in Engineering, Electronics, Computers & Digital Systems, Cum Laude. Kellogg School of Management, Microsoft Program Alum. Senior Product & Program Manager for Applications Platform at Microsoft.

His fingerprints were on technology that changed the world. He had worked directly with Bill Gates and Paul Allen. He had built, shipped, and shaped innovations from the earliest days of Microsoft through nearly two decades of transformation.

And yet, he opened with a sentence I'll never forget: "I think I've been set aside... and I'm no longer seen as an asset to my employer." This client, let's call him Nacho, didn't come to me looking for a job. He came looking for direction.

Seventeen years into a remarkable career, his momentum had stalled. A major medical crisis, a brain aneurysm he miraculously survived, shifted how others perceived him. Although his cognitive abilities remained exceptional, colleagues quietly treated him as fragile, limited, or incapable of the high-impact contributions he once led with ease.

He felt invisible in rooms he used to command. He felt underestimated in spaces he helped build. And the story he'd unconsciously internalized became: "I am stuck. I am frustrated. I am running hard...however, I'm getting nowhere."

For someone who had spent years being sought after for solutions, strategy, and execution, this narrative felt like a shrinking. On paper, Nacho's success was undeniable. He had achieved more than most professionals ever will. However, internally, he felt fragmented, out of alignment, overlooked, and undervalued. He had taken every step he believed he was "supposed" to take—engaging multiple coaches, completing assessment tools, seeking spiritual direction, and pursuing mentorship. Each offered pieces of the puzzle, yet none bridged the practical professional gap he was facing.

What he needed wasn't more data. He needed a new story.

The Moment of Agency

We began with what I call an identity excavation. It wasn't about rewriting his resume. It was about reclaiming himself. I asked him three grounding questions: "*What parts of your story no longer feel like you?" "Where have you edited yourself to be more acceptable?" "If no one was watching, what work would you choose to do?"*

He paused, then said a sentence that became the turning point of his transformation: "I've been living a life that's impressive... but not expressive." That clarity cracked open the narrative that had been holding him back.

Together, we mapped his story through a life-narrative arc: The Setup, a brilliant, curious child with engineering instincts and natural problem-solving gifts. The Disruption was a medical event that shook his confidence, identity, and visibility. The Turning Point, realizing he had accepted others' diminished view of him. The Decision, choosing authorship instead of acceptance. The New Chapter, reclaiming his strengths, voice, and direction.

The shift was immediate, not because his circumstances changed, but because his story did.

Rebuilding the Narrative

During our coaching process, we used identity-based frameworks to rebuild his narrative with intention and precision. We identified three foundational pillars that became the backbone of his "I AM" identity. Clarity followed, and confidence rose. We mapped his strengths to key leader archetypes derived from the CVI: The Visionary (Idea Scout), The Guide (Strategic Engager), and The Disruptor (Clarity Architect). He saw himself again, not as diminished, but as dynamic.

We recalibrated how he communicated his value by rewriting his resume, updating his bio, and reframing his narrative to gain cross-functional influence. Instead of talking about what he had done, he began speaking from who he is. Nacho didn't need to leave Microsoft to reclaim his impact. He needed to reclaim his identity.

Within months, he became a leader in several cross-functional communities, influenced a significant product launch roadmap, articulated a vision so clearly that he secured resources for high-impact initiatives, and reinforced balance across his life: spiritual, relationships, and career. Colleagues noticed the change immediately. He wasn't just performing differently. He was showing up differently.

His story had shifted from "I am stuck" to "I AM an Idea Scout, Strategic Engager, and Clarity Architect."

Nacho stopped waiting for someone else to tell him who he was. He chose his identity and stepped into it with authority.

> **"Nacho stopped waiting for someone else to tell him who he was."**

Crafting a Compelling New Narrative

The truth is that *narrative is currency. How* we tell our story directly impacts how we're seen, how doors open, and whether we're even considered for the rooms we deserve to be in.

However, this isn't about slick pitches or social media headlines. This is about **authentic, aligned storytelling**, grounded in truth and spoken with conviction.

Why Your Career Story is Running the Show

Every career has a storyline. Most people just never stop to examine the script. Dr. McAdams's research shows that identity is not formed solely by personality traits. Identity is formed through story, how you interpret pivotal moments, setbacks, successes, and turning points across time.

> **"Identity is formed through story."**

Your career story integrates your reconstructed past (what you believe happened and why), your experienced present (how you see yourself now), and your imagined future (what you believe is possible). This story becomes your operating system. And like any outdated system, if it's running old code, performance suffers.

By mid-career, many high performers are unknowingly operating from a narrative that sounds like this: "I followed the logical path." "I had to be practical." "This is what I'm known for." "It's too late to pivot."

These stories feel factual. However, McAdams's work reveals something critical: life stories are selective constructions, not objective truths. You choose which moments matter. You choose how setbacks are framed. You choose whether disruption is interpreted as failure or as a plot twist that advances the story.

When professionals feel stuck, burned out, or misaligned, it's rarely a skill issue. It's a story issue.

Themes of Healthy Career Stories

McAdams identified recurring themes that appear in healthy, high-functioning life stories, and they map directly to sustainable career fulfillment:

Agency. Stories where the individual sees themselves as an active decision-maker, not a passenger, are associated with resilience, motivation, and growth. If your story frames you as someone who "ended up here," you'll hesitate to move. If your story frames you as someone who chooses, momentum returns.

Redemption. In redemptive narratives, difficult experiences become catalysts for growth. Layoffs, stalled promotions, failed ventures, or wrong turns don't disqualify you. They clarify you. When reframed, they become strategic assets rather than liabilities.

Meaning and Direction. People with coherent narratives feel grounded, even during transition. When your story makes sense, decisions get simpler. You stop chasing titles and start aligning with purpose.

The Anatomy of an Empowered Career Narrative

Let's break down how a mid-career professional can build this new narrative:

1. **Own Your Origin.** Don't delete your past, reframe it. The goal isn't reinvention by erasure, it's reclamation.
2. **Name the Disruption.** Whether it's burnout, layoff, corporate disillusionment, or a divine nudge, this moment matters. Claim it.
3. **Identify the Transformation.** What have you learned? What new clarity emerged? What did you let go of?
4. **Declare the Shift.** Put language to your "I AM" now. What values define you? What work aligns with your essence?
5. **Point to the Future.** Invite your audience into your vision. Tell them where you're headed, not just where you've been.

Your Invitation to Re-Author

This chapter doesn't end with just theory. You now stand at the threshold of something new. Rewriting your story isn't just a career strategy. It's personal liberation.

Commit to truth over polish. Ditch the version of your story that was built to impress. Speak from alignment. Commit to visibility. Share your rewritten story on professional social sites (e.g., LinkedIn), in networking rooms, on podcasts, with colleagues, and in interviews. Commit to momentum. Don't overthink the first step. *Claim it. Declare it. Speak it. Live it.*

"Claim it. Declare it. Speak it. Live it."

You are not here to recycle someone else's dream. You are here to author your own. As Maya Angelou wrote, "There is no greater agony than bearing an untold story inside you."

A Personal Note

If you've made it this far, chances are you're no longer willing to settle for a story that fits a mold. You are not the sum-total of job titles or metrics. You are a whole human being with a purpose, a presence, and a unique way of seeing the world. **Your story matters**. And it's time to tell it, on your terms, with your voice. This is the **Claim** section of your life. You're not waiting for permission. You're claiming authority and stepping into authorship.

Elevation Practice: You Are the Author

Write your answers in the D by D - Interactive Workbook or your personal journal.

1. **Narrative Audit:** What parts of your current career story feel outdated or untrue?
2. **Ownership Check:** Where are you still living by someone else's definition of success?
3. **Story Rewrite Prompt:** Describe your next chapter in a few sentences. Start with: "The version of me the world is about to meet is..."
4. **Claim Your Voice:** What gifts and experiences have you minimized that you're now ready to own?
5. **Mentor Mirror:** Ask three trusted colleagues what they believe are your top contributions and compare with your own list.
6. **"I AM" Practice:** Practice stating your "I AM" statements that reflect your three pillars with 3-5 people who know you well and will be honest and objective.

Next Chapter Preview

Chapter 7: Discovering the Future You

In Chapter 7, we'll explore how to design your career from what you can do to what you are truly passionate about. You'll learn how to visualize your most aligned path, uncover the latent dreams you've tucked away, and begin building a concrete roadmap to make them real. We'll use tools from design thinking, vision mapping, and client case studies to help you create the next phase of your career with intention and purpose.

Chapter 7

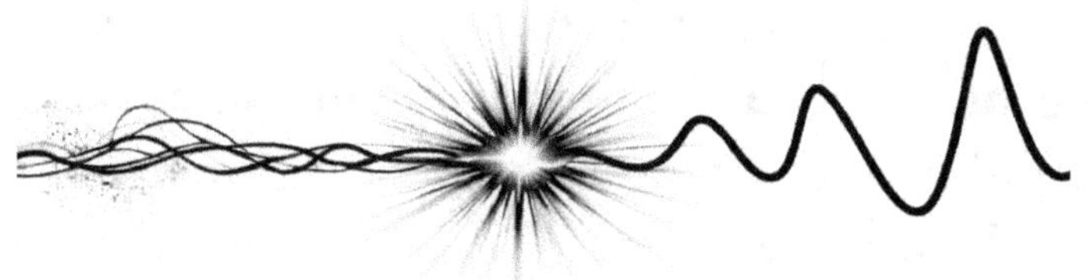

DISCOVERING THE FUTURE YOU

"Efforts and courage are not enough without purpose and direction."

—John F. Kennedy

Claim Your Core Offer

There comes a defining moment in every reinvention when the fog starts to lift, and what's left staring back is a simple, pointed question: What exactly do you offer the world, and why does it matter?

After navigating the emotional depths of disruption and the soul-searching required to reclaim identity, the next step is precision. This is where your *clarity becomes currency*. In this chapter, we move from story to strategy, from

"This is where your clarity becomes currency."

emotional excavation to evidence-backed articulation of your personal brand and career value.

Your Core Offer is the intersection of your genius (skills, strengths, expertise), your passion (what energizes you), and market relevance (who needs what you offer). When these converge, *clarity becomes magnetic.*

The Problem of Vagueness

In coaching high-performing professionals, one of the most common themes that emerges isn't a lack of ability. It's a lack of *clarity and confidence in communicating their value.* They say things like: "I've worn so many hats, I'm not sure what to lead with anymore." "I do a lot of things well, yet I don't know what sets me apart." "I'm great once I'm in the room. However, getting into the right room is the hard part."

This vagueness is often rooted in one of three internal challenges:

Attachment to the Past. Clients cling to old titles, roles, and corporate scripts as a proxy for their value. "I've always been the VP of Operations, however, I'm not sure how to repackage that now."

Relevance Anxiety. Clients are concerned about their relevance in mid-career, especially now that AI is advancing so quickly and displacing jobs once held by their peers. "I've always been tapped on the shoulder and asked to join a company, yet that has stopped, and now I'm not sure of my relevance."

Imposter Syndrome. When shifting into new territory, even highly qualified individuals doubt their worth unless they can point to credentials or external validation. "I know I'm capable, but why would they choose me over someone who's already done this for 10 years?"

The answer isn't louder self-promotion. It's precise articulation of what you offer and for whom.

From Corporate Suit to Evolved Entrepreneur: My Story

Looking back, neither the people around me nor I could have clearly seen the butterfly emerging inside me. There were early indicators, subtle signs of "what could be", yet no clear or straight line from a farm girl in Eastern Washington to a headhunter in Seattle to the founder of a transformational executive search and coaching firm.

But now, I see it clearly. The entrepreneurial instincts, the voice, the grit—it was there all along.

The Prototype Phase. This was me as a child, running mini ventures, asking "why" at every rule, *and believing anything was possible.* I sold candy from my Halloween stash. I made and sold crafts. I babysat. I looked for gaps and filled them. Even my 'mode of operation' revealed my internal wiring: I didn't just talk about action, **I moved. I made things happen.** I didn't ask permission to execute on a great idea.

I used to joke that Nike's "Just Do It" was my personality. In hindsight, it was a clue.

The Corporate Reality Check. Early in my career, I was proud to be part of prestigious firms such as Robert Half International and, later, Adecco North America. However, the tension slowly built. I saw inefficiencies in the system and found better ways. I developed a recruiting method that engaged in the "deeper conversation" and "relationship first" approach, yielding better results than the standard model. I was told to "keep it quiet" because it wasn't trainable at scale. Translation? "*Your effectiveness doesn't translate easily, and we don't know what to do with that.*"

The Catalyst Moment. It was my husband, Peter, who said it first: "Why are you working for someone else when it's you the business is following?" However, the call had to come from within, and in time, it did.

The Build. After nearly a decade with Robert Half, I was invited to build a professional services division at Adecco. It was a once-in-a-career moment: a global company backing me to start something new from scratch. I said yes. I built, stretched, hired, and fought for a vision that others hadn't yet seen, turning it into a thriving regional division in Portland and Seattle.

Five years later, in 2011, I launched The Schaaf Group, my own boutique executive search, coaching, and leadership strategy firm. Starting my own firm came with no safety net, no corporate marketing budget, no global brand—just my name, my values, and my deep belief that integrity, truth, and alignment create the most powerful results.

The Expansion. We grew. I began working with higher-level leaders, mission-driven organizations, and purpose-aligned clients. I built my executive coaching practice, *The Executives Agent™*, as an evolution of everything I had learned about alignment, branding, and career reinvention.
The Reinvention. The calling came again, not to leave what I had built, yet to expand it. To go from impactful to exponential. That meant completing this book, fully launching executive coaching, offering masterclasses, courses, speaking, podcasts, and exclusive client work in a new way. It was no longer about just serving clients. It was about serving a movement. This movement is a mission to help others reclaim their identity, rise to higher elevations in life with a renewed vision, claim and tell their stories from a place of unshakeable truth, and commit to a new future. This is the very genesis of *Disruption by Design*, and the next evolution of *The Executives Agent™*.

Validating Your Core Offer: The Lean Reinvention Principle

Once you begin claiming your Core Offer, a new tension often arises: *What if I name it wrong*? This is where many capable leaders stall. They wait for certainty, confirmation, or permission. And in the waiting, momentum fades.

Entrepreneur and author Eric Ries, best known for *The Lean Startup*, offers a critical reframe: Progress is built on learning, not certainty. When the future is unclear—and reinvention always is—the goal is not to be right immediately. The goal is to learn deliberately and move forward with intention.

Most professionals treat reinvention as a one-time declaration: "This is who I am now." That pressure often leads to overthinking or retreat. Ries approaches identity differently. He treats direction as a **hypothesis**, something to be tested, refined, and strengthened through real-world engagement. This doesn't weaken conviction. **It builds confidence through evidence**.

Once clients begin to name their Core Offer, a new tension often appears. "What if I get it wrong?" I see this moment all the time with high-capacity leaders. The instinct is to wait until everything is perfectly defined before stepping forward. Yet clarity rarely arrives through isolation. It arrives through movement.

Entrepreneur Eric Ries describes this as the **Build–Measure–Learn** cycle, a concept originally designed for startups. However, I've found it applies just as powerfully to personal reinvention. Instead of treating your future identity like a final declaration, treat it like a **working hypothesis**.

Build: Start by expressing the next version of yourself in small yet intentional ways. Test a refined positioning statement in conversations. Accept a stretch responsibility. Speak, write, or lead from a new perspective that reflects who you are becoming.

Measure: Pay attention to the signals. Are people leaning in? Are new opportunities emerging? Most importantly—does the work energize you or drain you?

Learn: Use what you discover to refine your direction. Sometimes you deepen the path. Sometimes you adjust the expression. Either way, you gain clarity through evidence rather than speculation.

"A pivot isn't failure. It's discernment in action."

A pivot isn't failure. It's discernment in action, a structured course correction. You keep the essence. And when leaders give themselves permission to move this way, something powerful happens: *confidence replaces hesitation*.

That's exactly what happened with Kristen.

Owning the Value You Already Carry: Kristen's Story

She walked into our first session with uncertainty in her eyes and a resume that didn't seem to fit the mold for the kinds of roles she dreamed of. On paper, her background was patchy. There were gaps. There were pivots. There were scars from a past she wasn't sure she could fully speak about, at least not in a room full of executives. And in that space, I saw something different. I saw **possibility**. I saw **purpose that had been earned the hard way**.

Kristen's story was raw and honest. She had experienced deep personal struggles in her past, ones that left her feeling disqualified from leadership in most rooms. Yet she had a fire in her heart for youth, especially those society saw as "too broken" to restore. She wanted to lead in a mission-driven organization, to do work that mattered at a soul level, and simply didn't know how to position her value or connect the dots for hiring leaders.

When she came to me, she wasn't just looking for career advice. She was looking for *permission to rise*, to own the journey she had walked, and to **claim** that it made her *more ready, not less.*

The truth was: Kristen had done the work. She had invested in healing. She had led from behind the scenes. She had served tirelessly in volunteer roles, community boards, and mentorship capacities. However, her professional narrative didn't reflect the depth of her strength, passion, or spiritual leadership.

She didn't need a resume refresh. She needed an identity reclamation.

We worked together through the *Disruption by Design* framework to unpack not only her experience but also her *essence and passion*. What did she believe in? What did she carry that couldn't be taught in a classroom or certified with a credential? And most importantly, what had life trained her to see, know, and lead through in a way that others couldn't?

Together, we clarified her "I AM" identity, not based on what others expected, however, on what she had been uniquely equipped for. We reframed her narrative so that her past was no longer something she needed to hide, yet instead, a source of power that positioned her as the ideal transformational leader. We redefined her brand, communication, and presence to align with the high-trust, emotionally intelligent leader she was becoming.

We crafted a leadership story that wasn't just about "experience"; it was about calling. She didn't need to contort herself into traditional corporate molds. She needed to **own her truth, speak it confidently**, and walk into rooms with the **authority** of someone who had **lived** her mission.

Kristen landed a role as Director of Philanthropy and Engagement Officer at a faith-based nonprofit school for at-risk teens—an organization whose mission mirrored her own story of redemption and renewal. The selection was a perfect alignment.

She brought strategy, empathy, and executive presence to the role, while also showing up as a living testimony to what transformation and advocacy could look like. Her ability to build authentic connections with donors wasn't just a skill; it was a *lived conviction*.

However, her story didn't stop there. After gaining traction, confidence, and powerful results in her first leadership role, Kristen came back for another round of coaching. She felt the nudge, that holy unrest, that something bigger was calling her forward. We re-entered the "Claim" phase of her journey, this time with boldness and a greater vision.

Within months, Kristen landed her dream role: Executive Director of a Global Lifesaving Organization, a position that allowed her to influence policy and community outreach, and shape messaging that advocated for life, faith, hope, family, and dignity.

What was once unthinkable had become undeniable. She went from unsure to unstoppable, from overlooked to in-demand.

Her most significant transformation wasn't external. It wasn't the job title, the network, or even the international reach. It was internal ownership. She stopped asking if she belonged. She began to believe she was sent.

Now, Kristen doesn't just have a leadership seat. She hosts it for others. She's mentoring women, building leadership pipelines, and telling the next generation: "You don't have to hide your story to lead. In fact, ***that's what makes you unstoppable***."

In addition, Kristen's story illustrates something I see repeatedly with high-capacity leaders. The transformation rarely begins with a new title. It begins when someone finally claims the value they have been carrying all along.

When identity, idea, and impact align, authority follows. And that's the real work of claiming your Core Offer.

Why Most Professionals Plateau

It's rarely a lack of skill. It's not even a lack of opportunity. It's a breakdown at the intersection of ***identity and articulation***.

What I've seen time and again in my coaching practice is this: High-capacity leaders often undervalue their most catalytic offerings. Why? Because they come so naturally, they assume everyone can do them; they've been told to focus on their resume bullets rather than their impact, because their story has never been reframed through the lens of transformation and value delivery. Because somewhere along the way, they stopped asking the question: *What am I actually here to do?*

Until that question is wrestled with and answered, it's impossible to make strategic moves that truly align with purpose, legacy, and fulfillment.

The Real Definition of a Core Offer

This is not your elevator pitch. This is not your tagline. This is not your job title or even your skill set. **Your Core Offer is the unique, valuable, and transformational presence you bring to every room you enter.**

It's the synthesis of your **convictions** (what do you believe is worth fighting for?), your **competence** (what do you do with excellence, ease, and instinct?), your **credibility** (what do others consistently trust you to deliver?), and your **calling** (what do you feel uniquely assigned to build or protect?).

When we distill these, we arrive at a personal brand that's not manufactured; it's *activated*. And when your career becomes an expression of your core offer, not a container for your credentials, that's when the real momentum begins.

Disruption – Designed: The Power of Clarity to *Claiming*

Let's pause here and name something clearly. This work is not about **reinvention for the sake of *"marketing"***. It's about becoming so clear, so grounded, and so confident in who you actually are that your very presence disrupts the status quo. You confidently ***claim*** the renewed person you choose to share, not default to offer. This is ***Disruption by Design***. It's not loud, not performative, not another polished professional persona. It's the quiet authority of a leader who knows their assignment (calling) and walks in it fully.

The world does not need more professionals following prescribed scripts.It needs *activated leaders* who understand their calling and bring it into every room they enter.

The Thought Leadership Lens: From Experience to Distinction

At this stage of reinvention, most people make a critical mistake. They try to describe everything they can do, instead of naming the one thing they're here to lead. Author and strategist Dorie Clark calls this your breakthrough idea—the intersection of what you know deeply, what you see differently, and what the market hasn't fully articulated yet. Thought leadership, at its core, is not about being loud. It's about being specific, relevant, and ahead of the curve.

In *Disruption by Design* terms, this is the moment you stop asking: "How do I market myself?" and start asking: **"What do I stand for that others are already feeling but haven't named?"**

Name Your Breakthrough Idea. A role does not define your future self. **Roles expire—ideas compound**. Ask yourself: What pattern do I consistently see that others miss? What problem do people bring to me before they know how to name it? What truth have I earned the right to speak because I've lived it, led through it, or rebuilt from it?

Your breakthrough idea is not aspirational; **it's earned**. If your idea could easily belong to someone else with a similar resume, it's not sharp enough yet. Differentiation lives in specificity.

The Identity → Idea → Impact Filter

Borrowing from Clark's differentiation model, we refine your Core Offer using three lenses that must align:

Identity: Who you are becoming; your "I AM" pillars, convictions, and calling
Idea: What you uniquely think; your breakthrough insight, perspective, or method
Impact: What changes because of you; results, transformations, outcomes—measurable when possible

If one of these is missing, your message will feel hollow. When all three align, your presence becomes undeniable. This is the difference between *having experience and having authority*.

The Thought Leadership Positioning Statement

This is where clarity becomes portable. A strong positioning statement does not list skills. It claims territory. Use this formula: I help [who] move from [problem/state] to [outcome] by bringing [unique lens, experience, or capability], shaped by [earned experience, wisdom, or calling]. Notice what's absent: job titles, buzzwords, corporate fluff. This statement should feel slightly uncomfortable, not because it's untrue, yet because it's precise. Precision requires courage.

One of the most liberating insights from Clark's work is this: you don't wait for validation to name your value—your value creates validation over time. Your role is not to convince everyone. It's about consistently articulating and demonstrating your **Core Offer** until the right rooms recognize it. Social proof, whether through results, stories, speaking, or leadership moments, is not about ego. It's about *signal strength.*

Signs You're Ready to Claim Your Core Offer

Let's ground this with a few signs that it's time to step into a deeper version of your career:

- You're restless in roles that others would kill for.
- You're tired of being seen for your past success instead of your future capacity.
- You can sense you're being underutilized; however, you don't yet know how to reframe your story.
- You're constantly helping others see their value, yet you struggle to name your own.
- You've had whispers, nudges from others, that there's more, and you're not sure what that *more* is yet or how to get there.

If any of these resonate, you're on your way to claiming who you are becoming, and preparing to release the limits of a chapter that's finished its work.

The Real Test

If someone asked you tomorrow, "What are you becoming known for now?" Could you answer without referring to your previous title? If not, it's an invitation. This is the work of naming the future you want, before the world assigns you a role. And once you name it, with conviction, coherence, and courage, you no longer chase opportunities. You **attract alignment**.

> **"You no longer chase opportunities. You attract alignment."**

A Personal Note

When you claim your Core Offer with clarity, the world around you begins to adjust. Conversations shift. Interviews sharpen. Opportunities find you. It's not magic. It's resonance. You stop trying to "fit in" and start *standing out*—not because you shouted louder, but because you finally stood still long enough to be seen clearly.

Elevation Practice: Your Core Offer

Write your answers in the D by D - Interactive Workbook or your personal journal.

1. What parts of your professional identity do you feel most confident about right now?
2. When do you feel most energized in your work—what are you doing, and who are you doing it for?
3. How have you seen your gifts make a measurable impact in the past 12-18 months?
4. What are your top three professional strengths? How do they show up daily?
5. What parts of your current resume, bio, or LinkedIn profile feel outdated or misaligned?
6. What would your ideal client, team, or employer say about the value you bring?
7. If you could be known for one big idea, skill, or result—what would it be?
8. What story do you want to stop telling about your value—and what story are you ready to start owning?

Next Chapter Preview

Chapter 8: Declare the Future You Want

In the next chapter, we'll guide you in stepping beyond internal clarity to external declaration—making a bold, visible, and actionable claim about your future, and why this is a pivotal moment in the reinvention process. This is the point where insight turns into direction and intention becomes action. We'll explore how to claim your "I AM," moving from rehearsing your potential to announcing it.

This is the professional "crossing the Rubicon."

Chapter 8

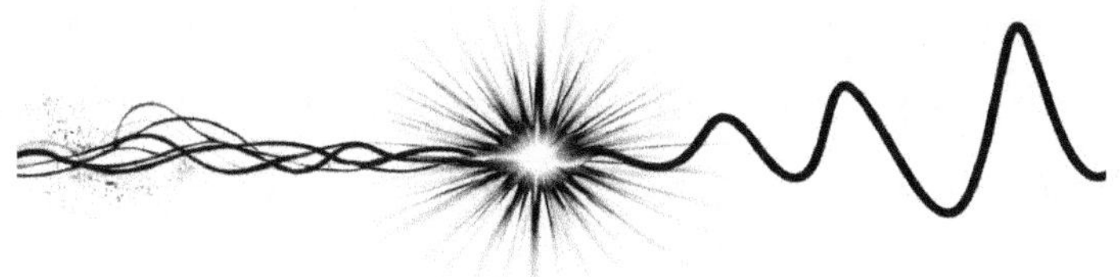

DECLARE THE FUTURE YOU WANT

"The future belongs to those who believe in the beauty of their dreams."

— Eleanor Roosevelt

The Power of Declaration: Crossing the Rubicon

Mid-career reinvention begins with an often-uncomfortable truth: we must stop waiting for permission to want something different. You may be holding an impressive resume, a polished LinkedIn profile, and a long list of accomplishments. And yet, deep down, you may feel unsettled, even lost. Not because you lack credentials or capacity, yet because you haven't *declared* what you genuinely want.

Too often, high achievers drift. They coast. They remain loyal to the paths they once pursued for practical reasons, not for passion. They wake up one day feeling like a stranger in their own lives.

This is where declaration shifts from simply being a personal or spiritual act to becoming a deliberate, strategic step forward.

To declare the future, you want is to own what you desire without apology, to speak life over your vision, even if no one else yet sees it, and to commit to action, alignment, and becoming the version of yourself your future requires. This isn't toxic positivity. This is practical power. Declaring your desired future creates a directional force that reshapes your mindset, decisions, and presence.

Why Declaration Works: The Science of Writing It Down

Declaration goes beyond motivation—it's a proven performance strategy. Dr. Gail Matthews, a psychology professor at Dominican University of California, conducted one of the few experimental studies to test how different goal-setting practices affect achievement. Her study didn't simply survey intention; it measured real progress across groups of professionals with varying approaches to their goals.

Here's what she found: participants who wrote down their goals were *significantly more likely to achieve them* than those who only thought about their goals. Those who went further—writing goals, creating specific action commitments, and reporting their progress weekly to a friend—achieved even more. The highest achievement didn't come from motivation or optimism alone. It came from *externalizing intention and creating accountability.*

In other words, writing it down turns a private idea into a public direction. Accountability, even as simple as weekly reporting, shifts your brain from "I want" to "I am enacting this."

A declaration that isn't written and shared is easily ignored – even forgotten. When you put it into words, action, and accountability, you increase your likelihood of follow-through not just by intention, but by design. Declaration isn't feel-good rhetoric—it is a strategic performance advantage.

The Cost of Indecision

Not declaring your future comes at a cost—a silent one. You may think you are suffering in silence, while it is **very likely** others are feeling your indecision in many forms, none of which are positively moving your life or career forward. There is a solution, and silent suffering is not necessary.

Every time you say "yes" to a misaligned role, stay quiet in meetings, or wait for someone to notice your contributions, you reinforce an invisible ceiling: the story that says, "This is as far as I can go."

You don't need another degree, another year of tenure, or another endorsement. You need the clarity and courage to name what you want out loud and claim it. As C.S. Lewis wrote, "You are never too old to set another goal or to dream a new dream." In my coaching practice, we call this the *activation threshold*. It's the moment when a client stops asking, "What should I do?" and starts declaring, "This is what I'm here to do."

The Stake in the Sand: My Story

People have often heard me say, "When you feel passionate or have clarity about a topic that truly means something to you, place your stake in the sand and stand firmly, with confidence and conviction." For me, that stake marks the moment a person stops drifting and finally declares who they are, what they value, and where they're going. It's the moment they claim their "I AM."

Clarity and conviction are in short supply today. Most people speak in recycled talking points, not truth, and leaders who hire can feel the difference immediately. One message is flat, forgettable, and transactional. The other hits with force—authentic, magnetic, and impossible to ignore. That's the power of claiming your "I AM" and bringing it into the world with purpose.

However, here's the rub: without a structured way to surface identity, most people default to the old playbook. Safe. Vague. Uninspired. It's no wonder so many interviews stall out and so many careers plateau. *Disruption by Design* exists to change that.

Rob's Turning Point

One of my clients, Rob, experienced this shift head-on. After we worked through the *Disruption by Design* process, he walked into an interview ready to own his identity rather than defend his resume. After he shared his "I AM" with the CEO, the CEO literally stopped him and said, "How the hell did you figure that out about yourself? I don't even know that about myself."

Rob told me this story with pride—chest open, eyes bright, energy high. He wasn't reciting a statement; he was living his transformation: confident, certain, activated.

That's *Disruption by Design* in motion; identity claimed, value communicated, future unlocked.

Identity in Career = Identity in Life

How we see ourselves at work affects how we see ourselves in life. Vocational identity strongly predicts well-being and confidence. When clients test their "I AM" with people they know, they get immediate feedback: *alignment and recogn*ition. They feel truly seen, often for the first time.

I've watched clients walk into our first sessions timid, unsure, or flat-out disillusioned. Then I've watched them rise—shoulders back, head up—because for the first time in a long time, they're building a future they intentionally designed rather than one they accidentally defaulted into.

Designing Beats Defaulting—Every Time

Choosing to design your life, instead of drifting through default settings, takes courage. Fear, imposter syndrome, and old limiting beliefs will all try to keep you in familiar territory. **However,** once a person claims their identity from a place of profound clarity, everything else snaps into alignment: goals, decisions, relationships, opportunities.

I know this because I've lived it. My life has been a series of intentional stakes in the sand: following my faith, leaving the small-town farm for a big city, pivoting from accounting to recruiting, navigating marriage, divorce, marriage again, stepping into motherhood, leaving corporate safety for entrepreneurship, and building a business from the ground up.

Each transition demanded a declaration of who I was becoming, and the courage to stand in it before I could see the results.

Three decades of serving, studying, and walking alongside people have taught me one undeniable truth: it doesn't matter how wealthy, educated, or successful someone is—every human reaches a point where identity must be reclaimed. Everything else eventually falls away. What endures is the clarity of your "I AM" and your commitment to living it out.

This is the heart of *Disruption by Design*: declare who you are, design your future, and pursue it with conviction. I've seen clients shift from doubt to opportunity, yet only after an internal change. Declaration isn't a job tactic; it's personal transformation. As Paulo Coelho wrote in *The Alchemist*, "Once you make a decision, the universe conspires to make it happen."

Tony's Bold Pivot

Tony came to me depleted. An accomplished IT executive at a world-renowned company, he had accolades many would envy, yet he felt invisible, "shrinking," and unworthy of more. He wanted to pivot into Product Development and kept hitting walls. Rejection after rejection chipped away at his confidence, reinforcing the narrative that he was "stuck" in IT operations.

In our work together, we flipped the script. We started by declaring what he wanted: to be a Product Executive in a prestigious, innovative organization, not because of the title, however, because of the creativity, ownership, and forward-facing work it represented. Tony said, "The three pillars were the most helpful for me. Once we identified my three core pillars, my "I AM", I lit up. "It was the first time I realized what actually felt real for me and how to look for that in my career."

He faced resistance, internal fears, and doubts about leaving the comfort zone of IT. However, he kept leaning forward, applying with intention, and networking with clarity, speaking from his future self, not his past resume.

The result? Tony landed a high-profile Product Management role in a global publicly traded company. He stood taller, laughed louder, and dated again. The work aligned. The finances improved. And perhaps most importantly, he had the clarity to prioritize what mattered most.

He spent irreplaceable time with his mother in her final days, something he told me he'd always treasure.

Tony's declaration didn't just change his job. It changed his identity.

"Tony's declaration didn't just change his job. It changed his identity."

The Neuroscience of Naming

What happens in your brain when you declare something out loud? Neuroscientific studies show that naming your intentions engages the brain's prefrontal cortex, the part responsible for decision-making and future planning. It also dampens the amygdala, the part that triggers fear and resistance.

In short: naming calms fear and activates agency.

This is why "I AM" statements are so powerful. When spoken with authenticity and congruence, they imprint a new identity on your nervous system. They create alignment between your beliefs, behaviors, and decisions. As Rudyard Kipling wrote, "Words are, of course, the most powerful drug used by mankind."

In my work, I've seen clients move mountains once they shift from "I think I want to..." to "I AM someone who..."; from "Maybe I could..." to "I choose to..."; from "I hope someday..." to "I am becoming..." This shift is not semantics. It's identity work.

Affect Labeling: Why Naming Emotions Lowers Fear

If you've ever felt fear lose its grip the moment you finally said it out loud, that's not weakness—it's neuroscience.

Dr. Matthew Lieberman at UCLA studied a process called affect labeling—the act of putting feelings into words. In brain-imaging research, participants viewed emotionally charged images and were asked to label the emotions they elicited. When they labeled what they felt, the brain showed a consistent pattern: increased activity in the prefrontal cortex and reduced activity in the amygdala, the brain's threat and fear-response system.

In plain terms: naming an emotion helps turn down the alarm system. Declaration isn't just about naming the future you want—it's also about naming what's trying to stop you. Because the biggest threats to reinvention are rarely external, they're internal states that hijack your nervous system: fear of being seen, fear of getting it wrong, fear of disappointing others, fear of outgrowing the old version of you.

"Declaration isn't just about naming the future you want—it's also about naming what's trying to stop you."

Affect labeling gives you a tool for those moments: name the emotion before it names you. Instead of "I'm stuck," try "I'm afraid of failing." Instead of "I don't know what I want," try "I'm anxious about choosing wrong." Instead of "I'll do it later," try "I'm avoiding discomfort."

This is not semantics. It's regulation. And when fear is regulated, you regain access to the part of you that can *lead, decide, and declare.*

Naming creates a handoff: from the amygdala (reaction) to the prefrontal cortex (agency). So, before you declare your next chapter, name what you're carrying in the current one. When you can name it, you can manage it. And when you can manage it, you can move.

Declaration as a Leadership Move

Leaders who declare with clarity create movement. When you own your "I AM," your team senses it. Your interviews shift. Your networking becomes magnetic. Your resume reads differently. Your energy in a room becomes electric.

One client once said to me: "After I started owning my 'I AM,' people started asking me to come speak, mentor, lead workshops—before I even applied for a new role." That's the power of resonance. People are not attracted to perfect resumes. They're drawn to people who know who they are.

If you're reading this and waiting for clarity to find you, it may be time to declare it instead. You don't have to know every step. You don't need a ten-year plan. You simply need to stand in your current moment and say: "I'm not going back. I am ready to own what's next."

Embodied Declaration: Why How You Stand Matters

Declaration is not only spoken. It is embodied. Social psychologist Dr. Amy Cuddy, author of *Presence*, explores how our physical posture and body language directly influence our internal sense of confidence, authority, and readiness to lead. When individuals adopt open, expansive postures—standing tall, shoulders back, grounded stance—they don't just look more confident to others; they feel more confident. They feel more confident in themselves. This shift happens because posture sends feedback to the brain about safety, capability, and control. While the original power pose research has been debated, Cuddy's broader work on presence remains widely supported.

In short: the body teaches the mind who you are being.

Cuddy distinguishes between performing confidence and accessing presence. Performance is outward. Presence is internal alignment. When people feel present, they speak more clearly, make better decisions, and show up with authority that doesn't need to be announced.

This is especially relevant during moments of declaration—*interviews, leadership conversations, boundary-setting, or naming your future out loud*—when fear of judgment can shrink posture, voice, and conviction.

You don't wait to feel confident and then act. You act in alignment—and confidence follows. When your body and words align, your message lands with credibility, your nervous system stays regulated, and others experience you as grounded and decisive.

"You don't wait to feel confident and then act. You act in alignment—and confidence follows."

That's not charisma. That's congruence. Before you declare: Ground your feet. Open your chest. Breathe deeply. Lift your gaze. You're not "power posing." You're claiming space that already belongs to you. Because *leadership is not only heard; it's felt*. And when declaration is embodied, it becomes impossible to ignore.

Words initiate change. Embodiment sustains it.

Elevation Practice: Declaration

Write your answers in the D by D - Interactive Workbook or your personal journal.

1. What future do you desire to create in your career? (Write in present-tense, as though it's already happening.)
2. What three "I AM" identity statements align with that future?
3. What external declarations do you need to make? (Think: telling your manager, reaching out to your network, updating your brand.)
4. What internal commitments must you hold? (Think: mindset shifts, boundaries, daily habits.)
5. Who needs to hear your declaration to help hold you accountable?

Next Chapter Preview

Chapter 9: Strategic Pivoting and Building Your Career Ecosystem

We shift from inward declaration to outward cultivation—learning how to pivot and surround yourself with allies, mentors, and communities that reinforce your future, not your past.

Section Three: Commit

TAKE BOLD, ALIGNED ACTION TOWARD YOUR FUTURE

Chapter 9

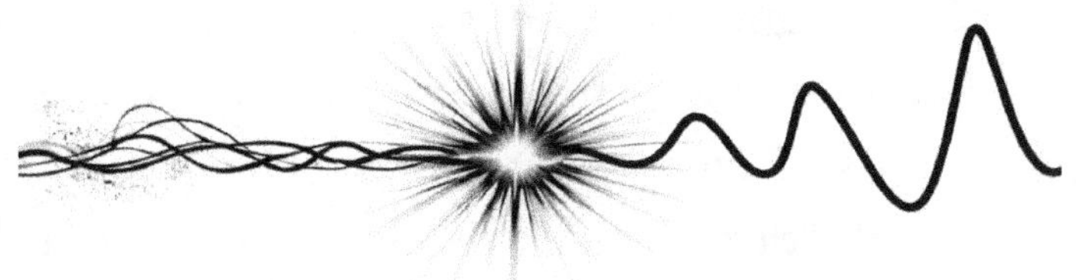

STRATEGIC PIVOTING & ECOSYSTEM

"Don't be afraid to give up the good to go for the great."

—John D. Rockefeller

Enter the Pivot Zone

At this stage in your journey, you've unearthed who you are, claimed your truth, and clarified your core offerings. Now comes the moment of truth: **committing** to action that aligns with your "I AM." And that action often takes the form of a pivot.

Pivoting isn't failure—it's design in motion.

Pivoting is a professional evolution that happens when your outer world and inner truth misalign. For mid-career professionals, it's not about abandoning everything you've built—it's about using your hard-won wisdom to achieve greater impact, alignment, and sustainability. You've outgrown the sandbox; it's time for the next thing.

What is a Strategic Pivot, Really?

With the context established, it's important to define what a true strategic pivot means for your career journey. We're not talking about jumping ship at the first sign of discomfort. A strategic pivot is a *deliberate, data-informed, values-driven* shift from your current direction toward one that better aligns with who you are and where you want to go.

It could mean shifting from corporate to consulting, from operations to thought leadership, or from people-pleasing roles to purpose-aligned platforms—moving from "stuck" to "in-motion" without sacrificing your credibility or confidence.

What it's NOT: a reactive leap driven by fear, burnout, or comparison; an impulsive escape plan with no clarity or foundation; or a shiny-object distraction from doing the real inner work.

Strategic Pivoting as a Career Advantage

Reid Hoffman, cofounder of LinkedIn and author of *The Startup of You*, offers a powerful reframe for career pivots—especially relevant in mid-career:

Your career is not a ladder; it's a living startup.

In other words, your professional life is an evolving enterprise, operating in a constantly changing market. The goal is not stability at all costs; it's *adaptability with direction*. Hoffman argues that successful pivots don't come from starting over—they come from **leveraging what you already have** while repositioning for **where the market is going**. Pivots are not erasures of identity; they are strategic expansions of it.

> **"Pivots are not erasures of identity; they are strategic expansions of it."**

ABZ Planning: Designing for Uncertainty Without Panic

One of Hoffman's most practical contributions is the concept of ABZ Planning, a framework designed for moments when certainty is unrealistic, yet movement is required.

Instead of betting everything on one "perfect plan," Hoffman suggests holding three parallel paths:

Plan A – Your current direction, optimized and executed with focus.
Plan B – A related pivot that builds on your existing skills, network, and credibility.
Plan Z – A fallback that protects your downside and preserves optionality.

Translated into practical application: for one client Plan A was launching her consulting practice. Plan B was a fractional leadership role and Plan Z was returning to the corporation she was working for with her newly clarified identity.

This is not indecision; it's *strategic optionality*. For mid-career professionals, ABZ planning removes the fear of irreversible failure. You're no longer trapped between "stay miserable" and "burn it all down." **You are designing** multiple intelligent moves forward, grounded in reality and self-trust.

Your Network is the Real Pivot Engine

Hoffman is unequivocal about one thing: careers accelerate through networks, not solo brilliance. Opportunities rarely come from cold applications or isolated effort. They emerge through **people who know your value, trust your judgment, and are willing to open doors**. This mirrors what we call your Career Ecosystem—the mentors, champions, truth-tellers, and advisors who help you see around corners and move faster with less risk.

> **"Careers accelerate through networks, not solo brilliance."**

In Hoffman's words, professional networks are not transactional; they are long-term alliances. When cultivated intentionally, they become the scaffolding that supports bold moves.

A strategic pivot means more than changing roles—it's *activating the right relationships at the right time.*

Why This Matters Mid-Career

Most professionals hit a point in their mid-30s to 50s where comfort becomes costly. You're good at what you do, but you feel misaligned. You're respected but not inspired. You're well-paid, but underutilized. This point is the pivot zone, and it's sacred territory.

The Pivot Litmus Test

Before pivoting, assess if it's time to shift lanes using the following four-part filter:

- **Resonance Check.** Does your work still feel meaningful? Are you lit up by what you do, or merely going through motions?
- **Identity Congruence.** Is there a gap between who you are and how you show up professionally? Are you shrinking to stay successful?
- **Impact-to-Energy Ratio.** Are you working harder, only to see diminishing returns? Is your energy feeding your work, or is your work draining your energy?
- **Future Forwarding.** Can you see yourself doing this for another 5-10 years with enthusiasm? What are you pretending not to know?

If you're nodding along—it's time to explore your pivot.

The Jump: My Story

When faith meets strategy in mid-air

Life is full of moments that demand a decision: stay grounded in comfort, or leap boldly into possibility. For my 50th birthday, I chose the latter—literally. I jumped out of a perfectly good airplane. Now, if you ask my husband, he'll tell you I'm a little crazy. However, anyone who knows me knows one thing: when Tina decides, she's all in. There's no halfway when purpose is involved.

Leading up to the jump, I faced the usual flurry of waivers—twelve pages of legalese designed to warn you that, should the parachute fail, the company would not be held responsible. Reading through those pages gave me a moment of pause. I considered the worst-case scenario. What if something happened? Was my house in order?

Then I asked a question that changed everything: "Am I jumping alone?" The answer came quickly: "No, it's a tandem jump, with an experienced trainer." That was all I needed. I smiled, signed the final page, and turned to the instructor with a grin: "I might as well jump!"

Van Halen's anthem has long been one of my personal motivators, especially when I am entering challenging rooms or roles. That jump became more than a birthday thrill; it became a metaphor for one of the essential pivots of my life—launching The Schaaf Group.

From Known to New: The Entrepreneurial Free Fall

Leaving a thriving company with brilliant colleagues and a well-earned reputation wasn't easy. I had deep relationships, a steady income, and a defined role. There was no drama, no toxic environment—just the pull of something more—a longing that wasn't being met, creating an incongruence with my soul.

I didn't leave because something was inherently wrong. I left because I felt a calling to build something that nurtured my soul, aligned with my purpose, and allowed me to serve in a way that used my unique gifts.

That's the nuance so many professionals miss: not all pivots happen because of pain. Sometimes, they happen because of potential.

"Not all pivots happen because of pain. Sometimes, they happen because of potential."

Still, jumping from a structured organization with built-in resources into building a company from scratch is no small move. Gone were the brand assets, legal teams, budget decks, marketing materials, peer huddles, and corporate shields. Every decision would now fall to me. I had to become both operator and visionary, builder and bookkeeper, voice and vessel. I had to jump—with no safety net—except the one I had built intentionally: **my ecosystem**.

The Power of a Personal Ecosystem

Keith Ferrazzi, author of *Never Eat Alone,* challenges one of the most damaging myths in professional life: that success is a solo pursuit. Ferrazzi believes: **Careers are built through relationships—not transactions, titles, or talent alone.**

In moments of strategic pivot, this truth becomes unavoidable. You do not move forward because you know what to do. You move forward because someone opens a door, offers insight, makes an introduction, or speaks your name when you're not in the room.

Ferrazzi reframes networking not as self-promotion, yet as **relationship stewardship**—the intentional practice of investing in people *long before you need anything from them*. One of Ferrazzi's most important contributions is this distinction: Transactional networking asks, "What can I get?" Relational leadership asks, "**How can I contribute**?"

This mindset shift matters deeply in mid-career pivots. At this stage, your value is no longer potential—it's perspective, pattern recognition, and wisdom. The most powerful ecosystems are built when you show up as a **peer, partner, and collaborator**, *not a seeker*.

Ferrazzi emphasizes that trust compounds. Small, consistent acts of generosity, sharing insight, making introductions, and offering support to create relational equity that pays dividends over time.

You build relationships before the pivot, not during the crisis.

This is why your Personal Board of Directors matters. These relationships are not casual contacts; they are

chosen alliances that provide perspective, advocacy, and accountability as you navigate change.

And when relationships are built with generosity, intention, and alignment, they don't just support your pivot—they *carry it forward.*

Talent opens doors once. Relationship keeps them open.

My Personal Board of Directors

I had been advised years earlier in my career to create a Personal Board of Directors. That advice became one of the most foundational elements of my success. Here's how my board carried me through the jump:

The Champion. For me, that's Peter, my husband, confidant, and the sound of reason and discernment. For over a decade, he had been nudging me toward starting my own firm. He saw something in me before I fully did. And while I stand by the belief that you shouldn't leap just because someone else says so, his unwavering belief was the wind beneath my wings. Everyone needs a champion in their corner.

The Cheerleader. John was a business associate who became a colleague, and he was a relentless promoter. He shared my name in every room, hyped my work without request, and did so with complete authenticity. Cheerleaders don't just boost your confidence—they expand your credibility in spaces you haven't even entered yet.

The Truth-Teller. Evelyn was analytical, balanced, and compassionate. She asked the questions that made me stop and think. She didn't sugarcoat. She challenged with love, dissected assumptions, and reminded me of my own high bar for excellence. Every entrepreneur needs someone who will help them get real before the market does.

The Herald. Drawing from Henry Cloud's *The Power of the Other*, the Herald represents a Corner Four relationship—one that combines high support with high challenge. This person sees your potential clearly, speaks truth without rescuing or controlling, and helps you stay aligned with who you are becoming. For example, a Project Manager/Scrum Master, in a team environment that is working comfortably, the Project Manager acts as the Herald by announcing a new project, a shift in strategy, or the launch of a new product. They are the ones saying, "The way we work is about to change."

For me, that voice has been the Holy Spirit. My journey of faith began on a summer day when a neighbor named Cam invited me to Vacation Bible School. That moment planted a seed that has never stopped growing. Over time, I learned to listen to God's voice—in business, in silence, in storms. The Holy Spirit became my divine Herald, speaking clarity when the noise tried to drown out my purpose.

The Expert/Advisor. Another John played a unique role on my board. As a business advisor grounded in integrity and faith, he brought wisdom earned from decades of guiding individuals and families through legacy-building. He helped me see around corners and made sure my decisions aligned not just with profit, but with purpose.

Purposeful Pivots Aren't Blind Leaps

When people ask how I knew the time was right to start The Schaaf Group, I tell them the truth: "I jumped, however I didn't jump blind."

My pivot was prayerful, strategic, and supported by a cast of characters I trusted deeply. Yes, it still required courage. Yes, it came with risk. However, it was a calculated leap—with the right people around me, the right clarity inside me, and the right purpose ahead of me.

Today, The Schaaf Group is a thriving consultancy celebrating 14+ years of impact, having transformed hundreds of professionals and leaders. I don't just coach others to leap. I've lived it. I've stood at the edge of a plane, stared at the sky, and decided: I might as well jump.

And the view? It's better than I could've imagined.

Megan's Pivot to Purpose

Megan came to me with a stature different from that of many of my clients. She was tall, commanding, and outwardly confident, exuding the kind of executive presence that might make an onlooker wonder, "What could she possibly need help with?"

However, once we sat down, the internal story behind the polished exterior began to unfold. While Megan projected confidence from every pore, inside, she was carrying deep pain. Her presence—formidable and focused—had, over time, created distance and tension with her colleagues. Rather than rallying champions around her, her environment had begun to produce adversaries, leaving her exhausted.

The cost was steep. The stress of being misunderstood, constantly defending her intensity, and feeling boxed in was making her physically ill, resulting in life-threatening health issues. Megan was no stranger to brutal battles; she had survived cancer. She knew grit. She knew perseverance. Yet the culture of corporate politics was draining her, and she knew something had to change.

Through our work together—using tools like the CVI, creating her custom "I AM" pillars, and developing her positioning statements—a truth began to surface—one that had been hiding in plain sight. Megan had spent years climbing the corporate ladder, playing the game, adapting her edges to fit the mold. And while she had risen to the level of Vice President at a global corporation, it had come at the cost of personal alignment and authentic leadership expression.

She wasn't broken. She was boxed in.

Together, we explored the possibility of pivoting out of the corporate hierarchy and into something that leveraged her strengths, honored her identity, and restored her health: launching her own consultancy. This wasn't an escape; it was a strategic expansion.

As we mapped out her pivot—clarifying her services, market value, and vision—you could see her demeanor shift in real time. Her piercing intensity softened into radiant energy. Her eyes, once focused like laser beams, now shimmered with possibility and joy. It was like watching a high-powered executive transform into a visionary founder right before my eyes. She was no longer seeking permission. She was taking ownership.

Today, Megan serves some of the same companies she once worked for, except now she's not sitting in meetings wondering how to fit in. She's leading them on her terms. As a consultant, she chooses projects aligned with her values, her expertise, and her designed future. She's no longer misunderstood or stifled. She's thriving.

Her pivot wasn't just professional. It was personal. It was powerful. It was designed.

What You Must Leave Behind

Every pivot comes with a cost. It may be a title, a salary range, a false sense of security, an outdated identity, or a hard look at what truly matters.

What you gain—alignment, energy, clarity, impact—is worth exponentially more.

This is the sacred exchange. Declare it. Honor it. Move forward.

Elevation Practice: Ecosystem & Strategic Pivot

Write your answers in the D by D - Interactive Workbook or your personal journal.

1. What type of pivot do I need to make (career, leadership, purpose, entrepreneurial)?
2. What fears are coming up as I consider this pivot? Are they rooted in truth or assumption?
3. Who is in my current ecosystem? Map your Personal Board of Directors by role.
4. Where do I need to upgrade or invite new support into my ecosystem?
5. If I fully trusted myself and my purpose, what would I do next?

Next Chapter Preview

Chapter 10: Leading with Confidence

In Chapter 10, we'll move from the moment of decision to the embodiment of momentum. After identifying your pivot and building the ecosystem to support it, the next step is execution—with confidence. We'll explore how to step into new roles, lead initiatives, or pursue your entrepreneurial path with poise, precision, and power.

Your future doesn't need more perfection—it needs more presence. Let's claim that.

Chapter 10

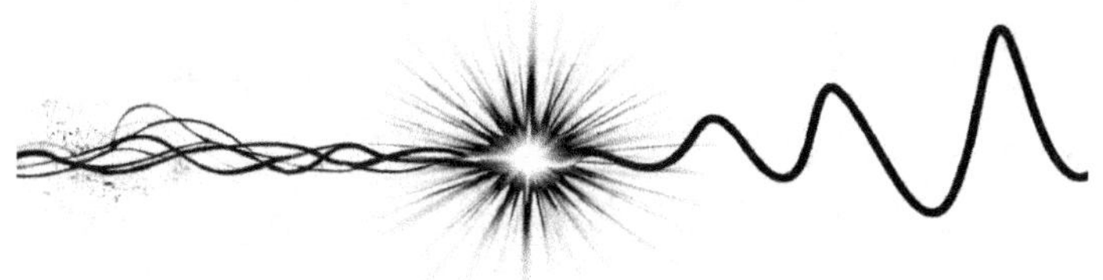

LEADING WITH CONFIDENCE

"Believe in yourself. Take on your challenges.
Dig deep within yourself to conquer fears.
Never let anyone bring you down. You got this."

— Chantal Sutherland

From Self-Doubt to Solid Ground

There's a moment in every transformation when things get real. You've done the excavation work. You've shed the masks. You've declared your "I AM." You've mapped your pivot. You've crafted your new narrative. Now, it's time to lead with it. Live it. Stand behind it without blinking. This becomes the ultimate test of your commitment—not just to a career strategy, but to *yourself.* Here, many professionals quietly panic. Questions arise: "Is this really possible?" "Can I speak so boldly about who I am?" "Will this disruptive approach really work?"

The answer is YES. When you believe in yourself and own your growth, you use your new foundation to speak with clarity. It's one thing to imagine your story in reflection. It's another to live it in boardrooms, interviews, investor meetings, pitches, or while leading a team.

Here's the truth: confidence isn't a feeling; it's a muscle. Muscles aren't formed by reading a book or making a vision board. They're built by movement, repetition, and friction. You lead with confidence by ***leading***. You speak from identity by ***speaking***. You design a different life by ***doing***.

None of that feels perfect from the start. This is about building that muscle; strategically, intentionally, and authentically, so that your actions align with who you now '*know*' yourself to be with renewed clarity. It's about ***showing up, standing up, and speaking out*** as the leader of your career and life, and what happens when you do!

Grit: How Perseverance Turns Doubt into Evidence

When confidence feels shaky, most people assume something is missing—talent, certainty, or readiness. Psychologist Dr. Angela Duckworth, author of *Grit*, would argue otherwise. Her research shows long-term success is driven less by innate ability and more by grit. Grit is the combination of **passion and perseverance over time**. Confidence doesn't come from knowing you'll succeed. It comes from continuing to show up when success isn't guaranteed.

Duckworth's work powerfully reframes self-doubt: doubt is not a signal to stop; it's a normal companion in any meaningful pursuit. What separates confident leaders from hesitant ones is not the absence of doubt, instead it's the decision to persist anyway.

Each time you take aligned action despite discomfort, practice your voice before it feels natural, lead from identity before it feels affirmed, or stay committed when progress feels slow, you generate evidence. That evidence compounds. Over time, perseverance becomes proof. Proof becomes belief. And belief becomes the solid ground beneath your leadership.

This is why confidence often arrives after you've already been brave.

Passion Anchors Perseverance

Duckworth also emphasizes that grit is not blind endurance. Perseverance is fueled by *passion that has been clarified and chosen*. When effort is aligned with purpose, people persist longer, recover faster, and grow stronger through setbacks.

This connects directly with the work you've done throughout this book! You don't persevere by force. You persevere because you know *why* you're walking this path.

That **"why"**—your **"I AM"**, **your calling,** your **designed future**, becomes the anchor that steadies you when confidence wanes.

Self-Efficacy: Why Mastery Builds Real Confidence

If confidence is built through action, the question becomes: What kind of action actually strengthens it? Psychologist Dr. Albert Bandura of Stanford University answered this through his work on self-efficacy. Self-efficacy is the belief in one's ability to organize and execute the actions required to achieve outcomes.

Bandura's research is detailed: the most powerful source of confidence is mastery experience—the moments where you take action, persist through challenge, and see yourself succeed, even imperfectly. Not encouragement, not affirmation, and not visualization alone. ***Experience***.

You don't gain confidence by avoiding failure. You gain it by **surviving effort and proving to yourself that you can handle what comes next.**

Another critical insight from Bandura is that mastery does not require massive victories. Incremental wins are often more effective; **they create repeatable proof**. Speak up—even when it feels uncomfortable. Lead a conversation you once avoided. Take ownership instead of waiting to be chosen. Follow through on a commitment aligned with your "I AM." Each small act reinforces a powerful message: **I can do hard things.** That belief compounds—and over time, it becomes identity.

Confidence is an Output, Not a Prerequisite

In the words of Tony Robbins, "Confidence: you don't wait for it, *you generate it*."

One of the greatest myths in the professional world is that confidence is required before action. The equation actually works in reverse: Action → Evidence → Confidence. You take aligned action. You see results or learnings. That builds evidence. Evidence builds belief. That belief strengthens confidence. And that confidence empowers bolder actions.

Too many brilliant professionals wait for permission to feel confident before they move. They want the strategy to be airtight, the job offers guaranteed, and the audience to nod in complete agreement. The most confident leaders build confidence as they go. They rehearse what they believe. They get in the reps. They practice saying what's true about who they are.

And they stop outsourcing their worth.

Confidence Versus Arrogance

Confidence is not arrogance, though the line between them is finer than most think. If you speak up and people actually listen, that's confidence. If they treat feedback like an insult, that's arrogance in a designer suit. If someone empowers others, that's confidence. If they take all the oxygen, that's arrogance.

The Three Cs of Aligned Confidence

Clarity. You already have the foundation: your "I AM," your core values, your career story, your strategic pivot. Confidence isn't about hype; it's about alignment with truth. You're not selling yourself. You're showing up as yourself. When doubts creep in, go back to your "I AM." That declaration isn't just a branding phrase. I*t's your intentional recalibration point.*

Claim. You don't need to be the loudest voice in the room or the most experienced. You do need to own who you are and be the same person in every room. When your identity is consistent, your credibility compounds. This is where daily rhythms and rituals come in. You don't just "show up confident" when it's time to speak on stage or ask for a raise. You *show up for yourself every day*, in small ways that build your internal integrity.

"When your identity is consistent, your credibility compounds."

Commit. Confidence comes from a decision, not a mood. Leaders act, whether or not they feel like it. Commitment says, "This is who I am. This is my work. This is my direction." You become unshakeable *by standing firm, even when it's hard.*

From a Defaulted Life to a Designed Life: My Story

There is a subtle yet significant difference between a life you "end up in" and a life you intentionally design. My career began as the former.

My journey to leading with confidence didn't begin in a corporate boardroom or on a big stage—it started in a vocational classroom in Yakima, Washington. During my senior year of high school, I was accepted into a legal secretary/paralegal program hosted at the local college. For me, this was the dream—the doorway to a legal career I had imagined since childhood. I even led the first-ever Legal Association of Students from our region.

During this program, I gained real-world exposure to law firms in both Yakima and Seattle. It was the mid-80s, and what I witnessed about women's roles in the legal profession was sobering. The culture was heavily male-dominated, rigid, and condescending. The path for women in law would be steep and filled with expectations that required my compliance and silence more than I imagined. I knew myself well enough, even then, to understand that my assertiveness, curiosity, and truth-telling would not survive in an environment designed to keep women "in their place."

So, I made my first major pivot: I defaulted to a career in accounting and finance. It was "safe." Respectable. Practical. Predictable. However, not designed for me.

Defaulting is never destiny. And fortunately, my story didn't end there.

The Invitation to Rise

Years later, I was unexpectedly recruited into the world of headhunting. I stepped into an entirely foreign universe. Picture scenes from 9 to 5 and the movie Working Girl—high heels, high stakes, and high intensity. That was the world I walked into.

Harkening back to my experience at Robert Half. I vividly remember those early interviews. I felt excitement, yes, and deep insecurity. What did they see in me? Was I really cut out for this? Could I thrive in a global, highly competitive environment with no previous experience in this industry? My confidence was shaky. And then something powerful happened. My father's words—spoken throughout my childhood—echoed in my mind: "**Tina, you can do whatever you set your mind to**."

I reached out to my stepmother, a woman who embodied corporate strength. Her response was pivotal. She asked: "Where have you already succeeded?" Her question stopped me. I took inventory. I looked at the evidence of my own life. The choices I'd made. The challenges I'd navigated—the results I had already created. She continued: "It is because of those things that I know you will succeed in this new field."

Confidence doesn't begin with hype. It begins with evidence. And that conversation gave me the internal permission I needed to step fully into the opportunity. So, I jumped—again.

> **"Confidence doesn't begin with hype. It begins with evidence."**

Discovering My Competitive Edge

Once in headhunting, I learned quickly. I persevered relentlessly. And I stepped into an environment that, by today's standards, would easily be labeled hostile. The pace I set didn't match the team's established rhythm, and not everyone appreciated the disruption. That was not my mode. My mode was: Get in. Get after it. Make connections. Make placements. Deliver results.

And that's precisely what I did. I mastered the metrics. I deepened the relationships. I created a system that matched my ambition and authentic strengths. And when I outgrew competing at the local level, I set my sights on competing with my counterparts in New York.

And I excelled. Top performer on the West Coast. Awarded Million-Dollar Club distinction for top-tier performance.

Those years forged me. They sharpened my instincts, refined my communication, elevated my relationship-building abilities, fine-tuned my leadership skills, and built a foundation so strong that it would later support two massive pivots: creating a professional services division for Adecco and, ultimately, launching The Schaaf Group.

What This Story Means for You

Confidence isn't a personality trait. It's not reserved for the loudest person in the room. Others do not bestow it.

Confidence is built—layer by layer—evidence by evidence.

It's created when you **stop *defaulting and start designing***, when you honor the voice inside that whispers, nudges, and urges you toward more. When you stop looking to the world to validate you and begin validating yourself. My story is not about perfection or polish. It's about ***permission***—the permission to lead, evolve, pivot, rise, and shine in the fullness of ***who you are called to be***. And if you're reading this, it's your turn.

Scrubs to Strategy: Elena's Story

When Elena stepped into our first session, she carried the quiet heaviness of someone deeply tired—not just physically, but spiritually. A seasoned healthcare executive with over 12 years of experience in hospital systems, Elena was the kind of leader everyone leaned on during crises yet rarely celebrated during victories.

She had built a reputation as "the one who gets things done," yet internally she described herself as "the ghost in the all-staff leadership room." Despite being one of the most effective operators in her organization, she often felt invisible, especially among louder, more self-promotional peers. "I'm not the problem," she said in our second session, "but somehow I'm never the solution either."

At that point, Elena was considering leaving the industry entirely. Years of being passed over for promotions and hearing, "You're not quite ready to lead large teams," had chipped away at her confidence. She didn't want to "fake charisma" or become someone else to rise. However, she also didn't want to fade out of a field she loved.

Using the CVI and "I AM" methodology, we explored what wasn't being seen. Elena's Core Pillars emerged with clarity:

I AM a Guardian of Dignity – ensuring patients, staff, and systems honor the humanity within the work.
I AM a Strategic Stabilizer – bringing calm, coordinated leadership in the most chaotic moments.
I AM a Transformative Voice – speaking compassion and truth where systems have gone silent or stale.

These weren't just feel-good affirmations. They were **truths she had lived** yet never fully claimed. With this new framework, Elena no longer approached leadership with a posture of "proving." Instead, she began communicating from a place of grounded authority—not loud, however, undeniably resonant.

Elena didn't exit healthcare. She elevated within it. She stopped chasing roles that required her to be someone else and began seeking opportunities that needed exactly who she was. When a regional health network posted an opening for Director of Patient Experience, she saw it for what it was: not a step back, yet a step into her purpose.

In her interviews, she shared her "I AM" pillars. When asked what kind of leader she was, she replied: "I'm the kind of leader who ensures no one has to raise their voice to be heard, because the systems we build do the speaking for them."

She got the job.

Within the first 90 days, she led a full cultural audit, implemented new staff feedback protocols, and helped reduce patient complaint escalations by 42%. More than that, her presence began to change the tenor of leadership conversations across the network. Peers who once overlooked her now asked for her counsel. Younger professionals started citing her as their role model. Elena didn't just lead; she became a lighthouse.

In our final coaching session, Elena said something that perfectly captured the essence of leading with confidence: **"It turns out, my voice wasn't missing—it was just buried beneath decades of being 'reasonable.' Now, I lead with resonance."**

This is what happens when we stop defaulting to how things have always been done and ***design how we show up on purpose***.

Growth Mindset: Why Confidence is Learnable

If confidence is a practice, not a trait, then one truth becomes unavoidable: **It can be developed**.

Psychologist Dr. Carol Dweck, author of *Mindset*, spent decades studying how beliefs about ability shape performance, resilience, and leadership effectiveness. Her research distinguishes between a fixed mindset, which assumes abilities are static, and a growth mindset, which understands abilities can be developed through effort, learning, and persistence.

In a fixed mindset, self-doubt feels like a verdict: "*Maybe I'm not cut out for this.*" In a growth mindset, self-doubt becomes information: "*I'm still learning how to do this well.*" Same moment. Completely different outcome.

Dweck's research shows that people who adopt a growth mindset take on challenges more willingly, persist longer when things get difficult, recover faster from setbacks, and build confidence through progress, not perfection. They don't interpret struggle as proof of inadequacy. They see it as part of the process of becoming capable.

> **"They don't interpret struggle as proof of inadequacy. They see it as part of the process of becoming capable."**

A fixed mindset asks you to prove yourself. A growth mindset allows you to become yourself.

Tools That Support Confident Leadership

If confidence is the engine of leadership, then tools are the calibration system—keeping you aligned, fueled, and firing on all cylinders. True confidence isn't bravado or blind belief. It's clarity in motion, underpinned by trusted frameworks, feedback loops, and internal alignment. It's knowing what you're good at, where you're headed, and how to walk into any room, or storm—with intention and conviction.

1. **The "I AM" Pillars Framework.** This is your inner compass. Your pillars should be rooted in lived experience, reflect your strengths and convictions, and serve as a north star for decision-making and setting boundaries. If you're not leading from your "I AM," you're reacting from someone else's expectations.

2. **The Core Values Index (CVI).** Confidence requires understanding how you're naturally wired. Whether you're a Builder, Merchant, Innovator, or Banker, the CVI increases self-awareness, explains how you're energized or drained in work environments, and gives language to your value.
3. **The Confidence Communication Framework.** This helps you fully communicate your Positioning Statement, answer "Tell me about yourself" with resonance and clarity and articulate your pillars through your career story. Lead with meaning and mission, not resume regurgitation.
4. **Narrative Reframing.** Every confident leader I've coached has had to reframe a part of their past that once caused them pain or doubt. Identify stories where shame or insecurity once lived, extract the strength and resilience forged in those fires, and rewrite the story from the perspective of power—not pain. Confidence becomes unshakeable when your worst moments become proof of your most significant growth.
5. **The Personal Board of Directors.** No leader builds confidence in isolation. Your PBOD should include a Champion, Cheerleader, Truth-Teller, Herald, and Expert/Advisor. When these voices are intentionally chosen, they become an ecosystem that reinforces your growth, encourages bold action, and safeguards you from self-sabotage.

Elevation Practice: Leading with Confidence

Write your answers in the D by D - Interactive Workbook or your personal journal.

1. Practice speaking from your "I AM" pillars in daily conversations and in the mirror.
2. Make micro-pivots that align more with your values.
3. Say no to one thing a week that pulls you off course.
4. Ask for feedback from your PBOD and let it refine you, not define you.

Next Chapter Preview

Chapter 11: The Courage to Be Seen

This chapter will unpack the personal and professional transformation that comes with visibility—not just showing up physically but showing up fully. We'll walk through how to recognize and dismantle internal blocks, embrace visibility as a courageous act of leadership, and express your truth unapologetically in rooms where it matters.

Chapter 11

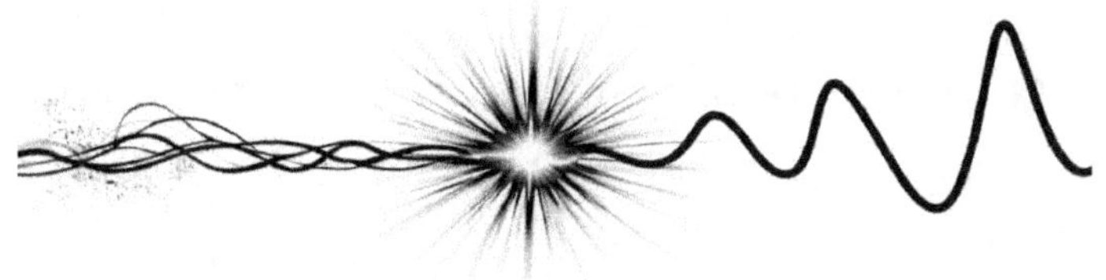

THE COURAGE TO BE SEEN

"Vulnerability is having the courage to show up and be seen when you have no control over the outcome."

— Brené Brown

The Cost of Staying Hidden

Invisibility has a cost—and it's steeper than most people realize. We trick ourselves into thinking that hiding is safety: keeping our heads down, editing our brilliance, muting our message, blending in. Yet each time we shrink to fit someone else's mold, we send ourselves the message that our presence is a risk rather than a gift.

Staying hidden takes many forms—keeping silent even when insight beckons, diluting your story for professionalism, dressing and speaking to blend in, waiting for permission instead of stepping up, taking roles where you're valued yet not fully visible. In each case, you gain 'safety' but lose authenticity.

And here's what it costs:

Influence—because people can't follow what they can't see.
Opportunities—because silent value rarely gets noticed.
Confidence—because disconnection from self leads to confusion.
Impact—because when you're hidden, you're not contributing at full capacity.

The takeaway: When we hide our truth, we stay on the edge of our potential, leading to burnout and a sense of missing fulfillment. Often, what holds us back isn't skill; it's how visible we allow ourselves to be.

Key point: Playing small doesn't offer protection—it erodes your confidence and impact over time.

Rewriting the Fear Script

Being seen takes courage: visibility opens the door to vulnerability. Real blockers that keep people hidden include **imposter syndrome** ("Who am I to speak up?"), **perfectionism** ("I'll show up when I'm fully ready"), **fear of judgment** ("What if I get it wrong?"), over-identifying **with role or title** ("This isn't what people expect from someone like me"), and **cultural programming** ("Keep your head down, do good work, and wait your turn"). Naming these obstacles helps loosen their grip.

These are not personality traits; they are *limiting scripts*. Scripts you inherited, absorbed, and repeated to keep you small or out of alignment with who you were created to be.

Here's the liberating truth: You are not your fear. You are the author of your next story.

Your truth, when delivered with clarity and conviction, is not a liability; it's your leadership. And leadership begins with ownership.

Naming the Impostor: Why Being Seen Triggers Old Scripts

When people hesitate to be seen, it's rarely because they lack competence. It's because an internal voice questions their right to belong. In Chapter 5 we explored masks. Here we look at the deeper psychological patterns that drive them through the lens of Dr. Valerie Young, a leading expert on impostor syndrome, who identified five common impostor patterns, not as flaws, but as learned survival strategies. These patterns tend to surface most strongly at moments of visibility, leadership, and expansion, exactly when you're stepping into rooms that matter.

- **The Perfectionist** believes mistakes equal failure. Delays visibility until everything feels flawless.
- **The Expert** feels they must know everything before speaking up. Hoards credentials to feel "ready."
- **The Soloist** equates needing help with weakness. Avoids collaboration to protect credibility.
- **The Natural Genius** assumes competence should come easily—struggles when effort is required.

- **The Superhuman** measures worth by doing it all—perfectly. Burnout is mistaken for proof of value.

None of these patterns means you don't belong. They mean you learned **conditional belonging** somewhere along the way. **Feeling like an impostor is not evidence that you are one. It's evidence that you are growing.**

Imposter syndrome isn't about capability. It's about how we interpret success, readiness, and worth. Imposter syndrome often intensifies **right before breakthroughs**. Visibility doesn't create impostor syndrome. It reveals it so it can be released. When you can name your impostor pattern, it loses authority. You stop treating the voice as truth and start recognizing it as an outdated strategy that no longer serves the leader you're becoming.

> **"Imposter syndrome often intensifies right before breakthroughs."**

Because the goal isn't to eliminate fear before being seen. The goal is to **stop letting fear make the decision**. When you own your "I AM" and let it be seen, you're not just being visible.

You've become ***valuable***.

From Impostor to Influencer: My Story

There are moments in life that whisper an invitation. However, if you're not paying attention, or if fear is too loud, you might miss them. For me, the pivotal ones didn't show up with fanfare; they arrived as subtle opportunities that required me to either step forward boldly or let the moment pass. One such moment arrived at the intersection of prestige and impostor syndrome.

I had been invited to attend an event at the Rainier Club, the oldest and most exclusive private club in Seattle, founded in 1888. For decades, it had been a men-only property, so exclusive that, until 1978, women could enter only through the back door on rare occasions. That changed when Judge Betty Binns Fletcher became the first female member, breaking the century-old gender barrier.

Fast-forward to the day I arrived. I rolled up in my reliable Volvo S80, surrounded by Aston Martins, Bentleys, and Mercedes in the valet lot. Walking into the walnut-lined entrance, sparkling chandeliers above me and powerful professionals all around, I felt that old voice rise: "*You don't belong here.*"

At that point, I didn't even have a name for what I was feeling; today, we'd call it impostor syndrome. However, what I did know was this: how you carry yourself matters. I'd already learned that the secret to being taken seriously wasn't just being present—it was being involved. So, when I discovered there was a women's leadership group within the club, the Executive Women's Roundtable, I joined without hesitation.

That simple choice changed everything.

After a year of active participation, the leadership team began seeking a new Chairwoman. To my surprise, I was approached and asked to throw my name into the ring. And while the invitation was an honor, my inner critic had other ideas: "Who am I to lead this group? These women are seasoned lawyers, judges, and corporate execs. I'm just a recruiter—how could I measure up?"

Still, I took the leap. I agreed to have my name placed on the ballot, and I was elected Chairwoman of the Executive Women's Roundtable of the Rainier Club.

With the title came new visibility and a seat at the quarterly board meetings of the entire Rainier Club, where I sat at the table with some of the most influential leaders in Seattle. Again, the impostor voice tried to pull up a chair: "You're the youngest here. They've done more. They've seen more. You're just... Tina."

However, I knew something now: I could choose to let that voice define me, or I could show up and redefine the narrative. I sought out mentors within the group. I asked questions. I paid attention. I honored the responsibility. And month after month, I went from feeling like an impostor to becoming a trusted, valued, effective, and visible leader within the club.

I was voted in to serve not one, but a three-year term, a testament not just to my leadership, yet to the power of choosing to be seen even when we feel underqualified.

Here's what I know now: It doesn't matter what zip code you grew up in, what college you attended, or what car you drove into the valet lot. What matters is who you are and how authentically, intentionally, and confidently you choose to show up.

And let me be crystal clear: showing up is not the same as just being present. Showing up is your voice. It's your vulnerability. It's your willingness to contribute when you feel unsure. Stop waiting. Refuse to sit out your own story any longer. Step in and be seen—the impact begins with one bold action.

The Trap of the Curated Self

Somewhere along the way, many high achievers become masterful at the persona game. We become fluent in reading rooms, saying what's expected, and anticipating reactions before anyone speaks. We are praised for it and promoted for it. Paid for it.

However, it comes at a cost.

Constantly curating your image can have consequences. When you focus only on how others perceive you, your sense of self begins to fade. You find yourself trading authenticity for approval, voice for validation, and power for performance.

Your curated self might get you in the room. However, your *authentic self* is the one they remember.

The courage to be seen means showing up with aligned confidence—not cockiness—and owning your story without apology. It means risking rejection in the service of resonance. And when you dare to lead from the inside out, you stop attracting roles that require you to shrink.

"When you dare to lead from the inside out, you stop attracting roles that require you to shrink."

Portfolio of Legacy: James' Story

James arrived at our first meeting under the impression it was just a friendly coffee catch-up. He had no intention of becoming a client. However, what unfolded in that casual conversation was something neither of us anticipated: a pivotal moment of recognition that would ignite the next evolution of his leadership.

James had built his career from the inside out of affluence. Raised in a successful family, he channeled his upbringing into serving the affluent. He founded a respected wealth management firm, structuring investment portfolios that consistently delivered high returns. From the outside, it looked like success. However, behind the polished confidence was a man quietly craving something more profound—something that aligned with his soul, not just his financial portfolio.

"I'm supposed to have it all together," he confessed. "But I'm starting to feel like I'm wearing a mask. My work performs, but I'm not fulfilled and feel disconnected from my soul."

James had grown weary of surface-level success. He felt the internal conflict between being seen as the expert with all the answers and the deeper calling he couldn't quite articulate—one that required more visibility, vulnerability, and heart. He sensed his clients needed more than financial projections. They needed guidance on meaning, on legacy. And to provide that, James would need the courage to see himself fully.

As we unpacked his story, strengths, and "I AM" pillars, it became clear that James had long curated a professional identity that kept him safe and respected yet also compartmentalized. He'd been showing up the way he assumed clients expected: innovative, capable, results driven. And while those things were true, they weren't the whole truth.

Beneath the tailored suit and market forecasts was a man with profound emotional intelligence, a heart for generational impact, and a gift for helping others make meaning from their wealth, not just more of it.

He had spent years maximizing client portfolios, yet his own "portfolio of life" was underperforming; misaligned, inefficient, and running low on purpose.

In our work together, James stepped into his whole identity. He rewrote his positioning statements, reframed his client conversations, and began owning his true calling: to help successful people design not just wealth, but well-lived lives.

I remember sitting in on one of his client engagements after the pivot. The man who once hid behind perfect charts and spreadsheets now opened the meeting by sharing a personal story—one that resonated deeply with the family across the table. That conversation led not just to an investment strategy but also to a family mission statement and a renewed relational connection across generations.

This became the new norm.

James' firm evolved from a traditional wealth management shop into a sought-after legacy design firm. He created frameworks to guide families through purpose-first financial decisions. His team culture shifted, too, as transparency, values alignment, and collaboration took root.

His firm tripled in size. He was invited to speak at high-level investment conferences, not just for his returns, but for his rare approach to impact-centered advising. Leaders started asking for his "secret." However, the secret was simple: he stopped hiding. James chose not to live a life of quiet resignation. He dared to be fully seen, and in doing so, permitted others to do the same. He became the light he was designed to be.

A Life That Reflects the Truth of You

When you find the courage to be seen—not just for what you do, yet for who you are—you tap into an energy that can't be faked and can't be ignored. Visibility is vulnerable, and it's the birthplace of resonance. Confidence is not charisma; its conviction rooted in clarity. Being seen is not about seeking attention; it's about stepping out of the shadows and leading with aligned identity.

> **"Confidence is not charisma; it's conviction rooted in clarity."**

When you hide behind old roles, past success, or people-pleasing personas, you delay your impact and dim your influence. However, when you walk into rooms with your whole self—your values, your scars, your truth, your brilliance—you become magnetic. Not because you're perfect, but because you're real.

"When you walk into rooms with your whole self—your values, your scars, your truth, your brilliance—you become magnetic."

And real leaders create real change.

The courage to be seen is the ultimate act of leadership, and the final permission slip is the one you write for yourself.

Visibility Without Volume

Visibility does not require you to become someone you're not. In *Quiet*, author and researcher Susan Cain dismantles the long-held assumption that leadership, confidence, and influence belong only to the loudest voices in the room. Her research highlights a truth many high-capacity leaders have felt yet struggled to articulate: **Introversion is not a confidence deficit. It's a different leadership operating system**.

Cain explains that introverts often lead through depth, thoughtfulness, listening, and discernment, qualities that are not only compatible with visibility yet essential to it. The problem isn't introversion. The problem is a culture that equates presence with performance and confidence with constant output.

You don't have to dominate conversations, speak first or most, perform charisma on demand, or compete for airtime to be seen as credible or influential. Leaders who listen deeply, think critically, and speak with intention often create greater trust, stronger followership, and more sustainable influence.

Quiet presence can be commanding. Measured words can carry weight.

Cain emphasizes that confidence grows fastest when people are allowed to lead in alignment with their natural wiring. When introverted leaders try to mimic extroverted styles, they often feel drained, inauthentic, or invisible anyway. However, when they lead from congruence—honoring how they process, reflect, and contribute—their confidence stabilizes.

Visibility rooted in authenticity doesn't require amplification. **It requires clarity and intention**.

Tools for Visibility and Presence

Visibility is not vanity. It's leadership. And presence is about alignment, when who you are internally matches how you show up externally, your influence expands.

1. **Visibility Inventory Audit.** Start with *what is.* Where are your strengths shining publicly? What platforms or conversations are you hiding from? Who needs to hear your story yet hasn't? This tool is a mirror, not a magnifying glass; it helps you observe without judgment and move with intention.
2. **The Presence Pyramid.** Build visibility from the inside out. The base is Identity—clarity in your

"I AM" statements and values that ground you. The middle is Intention—what you want your presence to evoke (Trust? Inspiration? Safety? Possibility?). The top is Expression—how you dress, speak, and show up in rooms. Most people focus on expression and wonder why it feels misaligned. You need to build up, not dress up.

3. **The 3R Storytelling Framework.** Nothing builds connection like a true story told with clarity and courage. Make it Real—share what's authentic, not idealized. No polishing to perfection. Make it Relevant—align the story to your audience's context. Make it Reflective—show your insight: What did you learn? Who did it make you? When you have 2-3 signature stories ready, you become magnetic.
4. **Your Visibility Ecosystem.** Map out your current reach, network, and influence zones. Include speaking opportunities, digital platforms, circles of influence – (personal board of directors), and strategic collaborators. Ask yourself: "Where do I need to show up more fully to match the mission I've committed to?"
5. **The "Seen" Habits.** Visibility isn't a one-time event; it's a practice. Post one insight on LinkedIn aligned with your "I AM." Speak up once in a meeting where you'd usually stay quiet. Schedule one visibility-building conversation. Say "yes" to one invitation that scares you.

Confidence compounds through consistency. Courage becomes character.

Visibility is an Act of Service

Let's dismantle the idea that stepping into the spotlight is ego-driven.

Being seen—truly seen—allows others to see themselves.

Your voice unlocks someone else's vision. Your story permits someone else to heal. Your presence becomes a pathway. Don't shrink to make others comfortable. Don't hide to avoid judgment. Lead. Speak. Shine. Because when you lead with the courage to be seen, others will too.

Elevation Practice: The Courage to Be Seen

Write your answers in the D by D - Interactive Workbook or your personal journal.

1. Where have you been hiding in plain sight? What is one bold step you can take to change that?
2. What story are you telling yourself about what it means to be seen?
3. Who taught you that being visible was dangerous or "too much"?
4. What would it mean to rewrite that narrative into one of courage, contribution, and clarity?

Next Chapter Preview

Chapter 12: Your Career, Reimagined

You've done the deep work. You've faced the discomfort of honesty, risen from default patterns, and made the courageous choice to be fully seen. Now what?

Chapter 12 is where it all converges. This is your moment to **shift from internal clarity to external creation**. You're no longer reacting—you're designing. You're no longer proving—you're embodying. You're no longer dreaming—you're declaring and delivering.

This isn't about reaching the bullseye once—it's about becoming the archer. It's time to step fully into the future you were made for.

Chapter 12

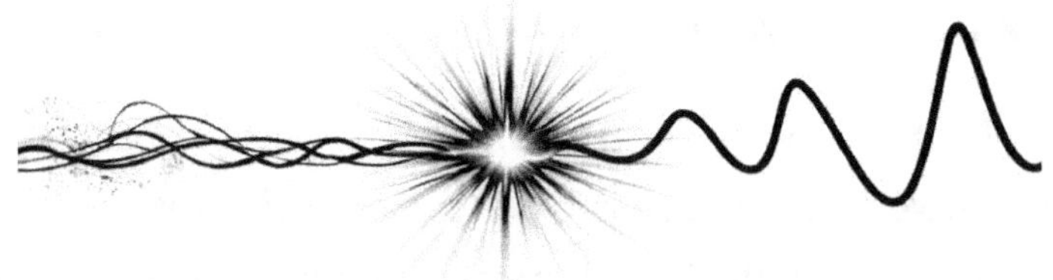

YOUR CAREER, REIMAGINED

"Success is knowing your purpose in life,
growing to reach your maximum potential,
and sowing seeds that benefit others."

—John Maxwell

The Bullseye is Now Clear

It started with confusion, tension, and fog. You likely opened this book feeling stuck or restless—successful on the outside yet misaligned inside. Maybe you couldn't name the ache, only that your version of success didn't match who you really were.

However, now everything is different. The path ahead is clear. Where you once saw an abstract target, you now see the bullseye.

You've identified your "I AM" identity through ***clarifying***. You've moved from living on default to living by design and ***claimed***. You've reclaimed a vision that feels authentic, aligned, magnetic, and ***committed***.

This is the bullseye moment!

Everything before this has been sharpening your arrows—excavation, clarity, reflection, disruption, design. Now, as you reach this chapter, it's time to aim. Unlike earlier sections that introduced new concepts, this chapter is about anchoring what's been revealed and making the conscious decision to live this career from the inside out, every day—not just during a job transition or a self-help phase.

Because here's the truth: Transformation isn't a one-time pivot. It's a sustained practice.

What the bullseye represents:

Identity—you know who you are.
Direction—you know where you're going.
Tools—you have the language, mindset, and process to support it.

Now, the question becomes: Will you take aim every single day? Will you keep choosing design over drifting, purpose over pressure, conviction over compliance?

Reimagining Work as a Lifestyle of Alignment

Let's flip the script: You don't exist to serve your career; your career exists to serve your calling.

That's a radical reframe for most professionals. We've been taught that careers are linear; that you get on the track, climb the ladder, stay within the box. And if you do that well enough, for long enough, you get a promotion and eventually a gold watch or LinkedIn badge of honor.

However, that mindset has long been obsolete. Today, success isn't about climbing the highest; it's about building the most aligned structure to your *life, values, and identity.*

Think Scaffold, Not Ladder. A ladder has one direction; a scaffold supports elevation from multiple angles.

When you reimagine your career, you move from narrow titles to multiple ways of making an impact. Influence isn't always positional; it's intentional. You stop asking, "What role am I qualified for?" and start asking, "What future am I called to co-create?"

The lifestyle of alignment means making decisions based on your core values, not just convenience. Saying "yes" only when it aligns with your "I AM." Letting success feel **custom-built**, not mass-produced. You didn't come this far to land a better job. You came this far to become someone new and someone true. Now it's time to live like it.

Choosing Alignment Over Drift: My Story

There comes a moment in every career where the question shifts from, "*What should I do next*?" to a far deeper one: "*Who am I becoming, and does my life reflect it*?"

For me, that moment arrived well into my mid-career. I had lived enough life to recognize a pattern most professionals don't see until they're forced to: Careers have seasons, and those seasons demand recalibration. What fits in your 20s rarely fits in your 40s. Values shift. Responsibilities deepen. Wisdom accumulates. And the person you're becoming often outgrows the life you designed years earlier.

I had reached that threshold. My kids were preparing to graduate high school and had already declared that warmer weather, not Washington rain, would shape their future. My husband had been ready for sunnier climates long before the rest of us, and after decades in the Pacific Northwest, he was craving light, expansion, and warmth. Their clarity made something unavoidable: a season shift was coming, and I felt the tremor of it long before I admitted it out loud. And like every human being, I felt the discomfort of change.

The Resistance to Change—Even When You're "Ready"

Humans love comfort, even when misaligned. I was no exception. We all cling to the familiar because it's safe, even if it costs vitality. Research shows 70% of transformation efforts fail due to resistance (McKinsey). People feel losses 2–3 times as strongly as gains (Kahneman & Tversky). And 40% stay in the wrong job simply because "it's what I've always done."

I was living proof of this.

While planning our relocation, I created the most elegant version of denial: a plan to split my life between two states—keep serving Pacific Northwest clients, retain familiar routines, nurture deep friendships, participate in community groups, keep a Seattle footprint, keep my comfort, even if it meant sacrificing presence with my family. It was "manageable." It was "logical." It was "practical." However, it wasn't aligned.

It was drift disguised as discipline.

When God Interrupted My Drift

Whether you name this voice God, intuition, or your highest self, there comes a point where the voice of truth becomes undeniable. I call it what it was for me: the Holy Spirit stepping into my denial and saying, "Enough."

The message wasn't gentle. It wasn't vague. It wasn't optional. It was clear, unmistakable, and direct: *"Go be with your husband and your family. Build what I've already placed within you. Stop playing small. Finish the book I gave you 10 years ago. My people need your message: Who you were created to be matters. You matter. And there is so much more."*

This was a total reorientation—a shift from drifting through life to intentionally designing it. Stepping into this new season, I realized: Transformation is not a one-time event, it's a daily **lifestyle.**

"Transformation is not a one-time event, it's a daily lifestyle."

My Daily Alignment Framework

To align with this new calling, I knew I needed to upgrade the operating system of my life. Not tweak it, but transform it. I rebuilt my days from the ground up, designing rhythms that supported longevity, clarity, and impact. These practices became structured, and then they became sacred. My new daily commitment raised my standard, sharpened my clarity, and aligned my life with my calling.

Wake with gratitude. Before my feet hit the floor, a big smile and a moment of acknowledgment: I woke up today. There is purpose waiting for me.
Hydrate with intention. Water immediately, to signal vitality and readiness.
Invest in others first. Daily blessings and prayers shared with the people whose lives I choose to pour into, a practice of outward focus before inward ambition.
Ten minutes of movement with motivation and gratitude: Five minutes of motivational activation and five minutes of deep gratitude meditation. This routine awakens memories, softens emotions, and brings clarity.
Strengthen the body. 30-60 minutes of exercise that reinforces flexibility, tone, mobility, and strength.
Cold plunge. A 3-minute immersion in 42-degree water. Courage practiced physically becomes courage practiced professionally. Your ability to own your mental state with an enhancement of increased release of endorphins,

dopamine and norepinephrine, boosting mood and alertness.

Devotion and prayer with my husband. Aligning spiritually before aligning strategically. **Hydrate again, continually throughout the day with minerals and peptides for peak performance.** This isn't just a "morning routine." It's a lifestyle of alignment—an ecosystem of habits and beliefs that supports your calling over comfort, anchoring mind, body, and spirit.

Life-Changing Alignment Through Small Habits

Life-changing alignment doesn't come from a single bold decision. It grows as small, intentional actions reinforce that decision each day. In *Atomic Habits*, author James Clear makes a deceptively simple yet powerful claim: Small improvements, consistently applied, compound into remarkable results. He calls this the **principle of 1% improvements**—the idea that getting just a little better each day doesn't feel dramatic in the moment, however, over time produces exponential transformation.

This is precisely why alignment, once chosen, must be practiced.

One of Clear's main points is identity-based habits. Rather than focus on outcomes, focus on who you are becoming. Habits are not tasks; they are votes for your identity. When you act in line with your "I AM," you reinforce self-trust, stabilize clarity, reduce friction, and make alignment your default.

"When you act in line with your 'I AM,' you reinforce self-trust, stabilize clarity, reduce friction, and make alignment your default."

You don't rise to the level of your goals. You fall to the level of your systems.

Clear also introduces habit stacking—linking new habits to existing ones so alignment becomes automatic. Pair reflection with your morning routine, anchor prayer to habits you already keep, or link courage to a weekly action. Stop relying on willpower; embed alignment into your life. Transformation is sustained by faithful, repeated action, not just dramatic moments.

From System Drowning to Courageous Alignment

One of my clients, a healthcare executive, came to me after her hospital merged with a for-profit system. Her role was changing, and so was the culture. She was considering a lateral move just to "stay safe." However, in coaching, she reconnected with her true driver: advocacy for patient-centered care. That clarity gave her the courage to say no to the role and instead co-found a nonprofit addressing healthcare equity. Her decision wasn't safe, yet it was aligned.

Tools for Career Reinvention

When you reach the threshold of reimagining your career, the most common mistake is to believe you need to start from scratch. That's a lie. Reinvention doesn't mean rejecting your past; it means **integrating with intention**. You're not discarding what you've built; you're **elevating it** to meet the future you've chosen.

1. **The "I AM" Framework—Your Internal Compass.** Reinvention begins within. If you don't know who you are, the world will keep assigning you roles based on convenience, not calling. Revisit your 3 Pillars. Audit every opportunity against them. Ask: Does this align with my design? Or am I defaulting again?
2. **The Career Positioning Statement—Your External Anchor.** This is where intention becomes articulation. If you can't clearly state what you offer and who you serve, the market won't know how to respond. Your positioning statement serves as the foundation for your resume, LinkedIn profile, networking conversations, interviews, and thought-leadership introductions. Revisit this every quarter. Let it evolve with you.
3. **The "Future State" Vision Map.** This is your north star. Before you make bold moves, you need a vision that pulls you forward. This isn't just about titles or companies—it's about how you want to feel and what kind of impact you want to make. Build

this vision across four categories: Career, Lifestyle, Health & Wellbeing, and Relationships. Design your life. Don't default into one.

4. **The Career Ecosystem Audit.** Actively and regularly utilize your Personal Board of Directors. Career reinvention isn't a solo sport. Ask yourself: Do I have people in each role? Where am I lacking support?
5. **Courageous Micro-Moves.** The biggest trap in reinvention is waiting for the "perfect plan." You don't need a 5-year blueprint. You need momentum. Choose one small, strategic action each week that reinforces your desired future. Every micro-move is a vote for the version of you that's emerging.
6. **Anchoring Beliefs to Sustain Reinvention.** Transformation is fragile unless it's reinforced with belief. Build a belief stack: I am capable of change. I am worthy of aligned work. I am equipped with tools and insight. I am becoming who I was created to be. Write them. Speak them. Live them.

You Were Never Meant to Settle

You were never meant to shrink, to tolerate, or to survive the status quo.

You are here to live fully awake, lead with fierce clarity, and design a life that mirrors the truth of who you are.

You've done the work. You've reclaimed your identity. You've named your pillars, declared your future, confronted your fears, and dismantled the narratives that kept you playing small.

Now—**step into it**.

You don't need more credentials. You don't need another permission slip. What you need is already within you. It always has been.

Let this be your permission to **stop waiting and start becoming**. Let this be the moment you **stop drifting and start choosing every day**, with intention and courage. The career you've imagined, it's not out there. It's in you, waiting for your decision.

> **"Let this be your permission to stop waiting and start becoming."**

So, make a move. Take the stage. Write the chapter.

Because transformation isn't an event—it's a lifestyle. And your future is waiting to be claimed by someone bold enough to live it on purpose.

Elevation Practice: The Sustainability Plan

You see the bullseye. You know all the tools in your toolkit. You've recalibrated your belief structure from **default to design**. Now seize it. Transformation isn't an event; it's a lifestyle. Write your answers in the D by D - Interactive Workbook or your personal journal.

You are fully equipped to move forward, on your terms, in your truth.

Your 90-Day Check-In. Set a calendar reminder for 90 days from today. Answer: What have I implemented from this book? What's shifted in my career? Am I defaulting or designing? What needs to change in the next quarter?

Your Annual Assessment. Set a calendar reminder for one year from today. Answer: Am I where I want to be? Am I fulfilled? Do I have the PBOD around me that is helping to elevate my life? Am I meeting regularly with my PBOD, coach, or mentor?

Sign it. Date it. Own it. Let's go!

"You don't become what you wish for.
You become what you are willing to boldly build—
brick by brick, belief by belief, day by day...

Disruption by Design!"

— Tina Schaaf

CONCLUSION: THE LIFE YOU WERE MEANT TO DESIGN

You didn't pick up this book because your life was falling apart. You picked it up because something fierce inside you knew it was time to rise.

That knowing—the quiet nudge, the throbbing restlessness, the ache for more—was never a weakness. It was your wisdom. It was your relentless truth, the part of you that refused to stay trapped in a version of success that felt suffocating.

Throughout these pages, you've named the fog instead of running from it. You stood at the crossroads instead of numbing out. You stopped reacting to disruption and learned how to design through it. That bravery alone sets you apart in a noisy world.

You did the rare work most avoid because it demands honesty, courage, and ownership. You clarified what matters. You reclaimed who you are. You claimed your voice, your story, your value. And you committed—not just to the next move—but to **alignment**.

This is not a small thing.

You now understand something fundamental: Your career is not the source of your identity. Your title does not determine your worth. Your past success is not your future's limit. Your power has always lived in your ***I AM***.

When you operate from clarity instead of confusion, confidence stops being something you chase; it becomes something you embody. Similarly, when you lead from identity rather than performance, decisions become simpler. Boundaries strengthen. Opportunities sharpen. You stop asking, *"Am I enough?"* and start asking, *"Is this aligned?"*

That is what true leadership feels like.

Disruption by Design was never about blowing up your life or walking away from everything you've built. Rather, it was about **building on purpose instead of by accident**. About choosing authorship over autopilot. About trading the safety of the familiar for the integrity of the true.

Some of you will pivot boldly. Some of you will redesign quietly. Some of you will stay exactly where you are— yet show up as a completely different person.

Every transformation matters. Every act of courage is counted.

What matters is this: you own your identity. You stop waiting for permission. You distinguish motion from meaning. You know who you are. And now, the responsibility shifts.

Not to do everything at once. Not to have the whole plan figured out. However, to **live congruently**—to make decisions, large and small, that honor the truth you've uncovered here.

The world doesn't need more impressive resumes.

It needs people who are fiercely awake, deeply grounded, and fully alive to their purpose.

So, as you close this book, don't rush back to noise. Pause. Breathe. Stand tall. Ask yourself—not someday, but **now**:

Who am I becoming?

What am I willing to stop pretending about?

What would it look like to trust myself completely?

Then do the bravest thing of all. Live the answers. This is not the end of your story. It's the moment you stopped defaulting and started designing. Go forward with clarity. Lead with conviction. And commit to building a life and career that finally reflect who you've always been.

Your time is now—stand up, claim it, and let the world feel your impact!

Let's keep building the future—by design.

With boldness, grace, and belief in your rise,
Tina Schaaf
Founder, The Executives Agent™

ABOUT THE AUTHOR

Tina Schaaf is an executive coach, speaker, leadership strategist, and founder of The Executives Agent™ and The Schaaf Group. For more than two decades, she has worked behind the scenes with CEOs, founders, and high-performing professionals navigating the moments that change everything—career pivots, identity shifts, and the quiet realization that success no longer feels aligned with who they truly are.

However, Tina's work was not born only from observing others. It was forged through her own seasons of disruption.

After years in executive recruiting and business leadership, Tina began to notice a pattern. The most accomplished people in the room were often the most internally conflicted. They had built impressive careers, yet many quietly wrestled with the same question: *Is this really who I'm meant to be?*

That realization became the foundation of Tina's life's work.

Through her coaching practice and leadership advisory firm, The Executives Agent™, Tina helps leaders move beyond external success and reconnect with identity, purpose, and truth. Her work centers on a powerful belief:

most career challenges are not capability problems—they are identity misalignment.

Known for her clarity, candor, and deep intuition, Tina guides professionals through the process of reclaiming their "I AM"—the internal compass that drives authentic leadership and meaningful impact.

Disruption by Design grew out of decades of working with leaders at their most pivotal crossroads. In these pages, Tina shares the framework she has used with hundreds of clients to help them move from uncertainty to clarity, from pressure-driven achievement to purpose-driven leadership.

She lives her message every day: that the most powerful disruption in your life is the one you choose on purpose.

Continue your journey at: www.theexecutivesagent.com where you will find new tools, newsletters, workshops, podcasts, online events/challenges, speaker kit, and coaching experiences awaiting.

www.ingramcontent.com/pod-product-compliance
Lightning Source LLC
LaVergne TN
LVHW020714110826
845149LV00012B/2260

* 9 7 8 1 9 6 1 2 0 2 7 8 8 *